ANNA PARTRIDGE has worked with children and their families for over 15 years as a teacher, counselor, writer and parenting mentor. She is an expert on the theory of resilience in children and has combined this with positive psychology to help children thrive and flourish in a changing world. With the introduction of technology, fast paced, busy lifestyles and a noticeable dearth of resilience, families are riding a new wave and Anna has been grateful to be with them on this journey. With an educational background, Anna uses her knowledge of interpersonal relationships and emotional intelligence as well as cognitive behaviour theory to help families understand and develop solid relationships between parents and their children. She helps families understand that life is meant to be up and down and develops resilience to help them weather the storm. Anna is an advocate for children's mental health and wellbeing and a regular parenting writer for Huffington Post and the Wellbeing Magazine. Currently working as a high school teacher, she loves the rich conversations she has with teenagers about thriving socially, emotionally, mentally and physically and also enjoys leading a culture of wellbeing across the schools she has taught in. Anna is married with three children and lives in Canberra, Australia.

www.annapartridge.com

THE ART OF RAISING A RESILIENT CHILD

Raising children with a strong mind, brave heart and healthy body from the beginning

ANNA PARTRIDGE

First published in 2020

Copyright © Anna Partridge, 2020

The moral right of the author has been asserted.

All rights reserved. No part of this book may be reproduced or transmitted by any person or entity, including internet search engines or retailers, in any form or by any means, electronic or mechanical, including photocopying (except under the statutory exceptions provisions of the Australia Copyright Act 1968), recording, scanning or by any information storage and retrieval system without the prior written permission of the copyright holder.

Cataloguing-in-Publication data is available from the National Library of Australia.

ISBN 978-0-6487483-1-1 (print)
ISBN 978-0-6487483-0-4 (digital)

Front cover image: Canva images
Back cover image: Wendy Yalom
Editor and Agent: Anjanette Fennell
Interior design and typeset: Maureen Cutajar, gopublished.com

For Tony, Zoe, Lachie and Maddie.

Thank you for riding this journey of life and teaching me how to be human along the way. May your hearts and minds continue to shine.

CONTENTS

PREFACE 1
CHAPTER 1   What is resilience? 7
CHAPTER 2   The building blocks of resilience 17

PART 1:
Building a Strong Mind

CHAPTER 3   Provide a positive learning
            environment at home. 33
CHAPTER 4   Give your child the best start EARLY. 51
CHAPTER 5   Provide the best education for your child . . 67
CHAPTER 6   Develop a strong values and beliefs system . 79
CHAPTER 7   Build up a bank of positive memories 85
CHAPTER 8   Encourage a growth mindset and
            positive outlook on life. 91
CHAPTER 9   Build self-esteem and self-confidence . . . 101
CHAPTER 10 Facilitate an understanding of
            financial matters 115

PART 2:
Moulding a Brave Heart

CHAPTER 11	The Importance of Building Relationships: Parent to Child.	125
CHAPTER 12	The importance of building relationships: Siblings	167
CHAPTER 13	The importance of building relationships: A Strong Community	177
CHAPTER 14	Teach children about emotions	189

PART 3:
Nurturing a healthy body

CHAPTER 15	Start with a healthy pregnancy.	213
CHAPTER 16	Encourage sound sleeping habits	217
CHAPTER 17	Maintain good nutrition	243
CHAPTER 18	Children need plenty of exercise.	267
CHAPTER 19	Make good hygiene a habit.	277
CHAPTER 20	A typical day in the life of a healthy child. .	281
CONCLUSION	Call to Action	289

PREFACE

Throughout every corner of the western world, the mental health of our children is deteriorating.

Mental health is now one of the top three health issues across all age groups, along with heart disease and obesity.

Study after study shows that children and teenagers are suffering from high levels of anxiety, depression, ADHD and suicidal thoughts. The statistics back this up:

- One in four children in every classroom are experiencing moderate to severe anxiety and depression
- Australia is experiencing its highest rate of suicide in 13 years
- The suicide rate for girls aged between 16 and 19 years has doubled since 2008 with one in 20 attempting suicide between the age of 16-17 years in a 12 month period and one in six self harming
- Eight people take their lives every day
- The highest suicide rates are among men aged between 18 and 35 years

Alarm bells are ringing.

Questions need to be asked.

- Why is this occurring at such high rates in this generation?
- What can be done to curb the high levels of anxiety and depression that are ever present in our schools?

These are questions I ponder on a daily basis.

As a primary school teacher and now high school teacher, I have seen my fair share of the picture that is painted above and I know there is more we can do. I know that the children and teenagers of this generation deserve more from us as parents and I hope to be able to give you the information to navigate the challenges our generation of children and teenagers are facing and some hope that we can walk alongside our children and teenagers at this changing and challenging time.

With my eyes and ears wide open for the past 15 years as a teacher and mother, I have come to the conclusion there are seven major reasons contributing to the deteriorating mental health of our children right now.

COMMUNITIES HAVE DWINDLED. Families have become nuclear. There is no longer an aunt, uncle or great grandmother living around the corner for the kids to drop into on their way home from school. That lovely neighbour who talks over the back fence and watches out for the kids is no longer there. The local shopkeeper or corner store-owner is no longer there to ask the kids how their day was. There is no longer a village raising our children and so sadly the crucial conversations between adults and children are not taking place. Children are relying on their peers for guidance and reassurance.

KIDS ARE LESS EXPOSED TO RISK. Being allowed to climb a tree, play in the creek or ride a bike around the neighbourhood are a thing of the past. These activities provided valuable opportunities to learn to bounce back from adversity and develop intrinsic coping mechanisms. Now, our playgrounds are too safe. We are so concerned our kids might hurt themselves; we have built soft fall playgrounds and low monkey bars. There are no seesaws to smack you in the chin and no swings to go as high as you can. They are safe with no opportunity for risk taking.

THE PRESSURE TO BE PERFECT IS HEIGHTENED. There is little opportunity for our kids to make mistakes and improve. We are so focused on how our kids are doing in NAPLAN that we forget to see how they are doing socially and emotionally. Our kids are conforming to perfection and not taking risks to make mistakes, fail and learn. When they are so focused on doing it right, they loose the drive to do it at all. In addition, life on Instagram and Facebook is perfect – the perfect illusion. It is a highlight reel of someone's life, not real life that is lived in the up and down, sometimes both at the same time.

WE LIVE IN A 'HURRY UP' CULTURE. The pace of our lives has increased. We are constantly on a treadmill going from one place to the next. For kids, who naturally live in the moment, there is little time to play and learn or for us to teach. The number of children who cannot tie their shoelace at the age of 6 is alarming and it's because its hard to teach this skill when you are running out the door. More importantly, there is reduced time for the crucial conversations with our kids because we are running around so much. It is a rush to get the kids home, fed, bathed and into bed before we wake the next morning to start again on the treadmill.

OUR DIET HAS CHANGED. Since 1970s, with the advent of fast food and resulting changes in the make up of trans-fats and oils, our salt, sugar and fat intake has increased significantly. Along side this, consumption of fresh foods and home cooked meals have decreased. This is putting a huge strain on our bodies to recover from an illness and bounce back from disease. The obesity rates are massive – especially in children. Childhood obesity in the United States has more than doubled in children and quadrupled in adolescents in the past 30 years. In 2012, more than one third of children and adolescents were overweight or obese. Obesity increases the propensity to acquire cardio vascular disease and diabetes. It also decreases the ability to bounce back from illness, can cause bone and joint problems, affects sleep and self-confidence.

OUR LIFESTYLE HAS BECOME MORE SEDENTARY. Children are spending less time outside playing and are less active in general. Children are being driven to school instead of walking or riding bikes because it is quicker, more convenient or safer. Families are choosing to watch a movie together, rather than go on a bike ride or walk the dog. Children are not reaching the recommended minimum of exercise each day required to build strong healthy bones and bodies.

CONVERSATIONS HAVE CHANGED. A typical conversation for a teenager revolves around Snap Chat, Insta Chat or Messenger. In person conversations are not the norm for our teenagers, which makes it challenging to have a dinner time conversation or meaningful conversation in the car. The art of conversation is not practiced every day in the way it used to occur.

How can we as parents support our children in this generation?
Parenting is both an art and a science. In knowing the basis of what resilience is and how you can instill it in your children, you are preparing your children to be mentally well throughout the periods of childhood, adolescence and adulthood. By developing the build-

ing blocks of resilience from a young age, children can bounce back and weather the storm that is life.

We can build resilience, confidence and emotional intelligence into our children from the minute they can walk and talk. We can raise risk takers, instil good habits and build connection through conversation and authenticity. We can create a positive home environment that nurtures a child's heart, mind and body and we can teach our children how to navigate the ups and downs life throws at us.

When writing this book, I looked for answers in the school, houses of many families and turned to parenting experts, school principals, teachers and community members. I'm in a privileged position as a school teacher and mother and have front row seats to humanity seeing life in its many forms. I get to see the 'big picture' of raising a child. I get to see the traits a child needs to be ready to take on the world. I get to see all the ingredients that go into a child and the effect each has on an individual. I see what works for some kids and what doesn't work for others.

Children who have the strategies to cope with stress can navigate and bounce back. They know how their thoughts affect their feelings and their actions and they know how to use positive self-talk. They know where to go for help and when to get it. They feel like they are walking with someone throughout their journey of life, not walking alone in this big world. They grow into active citizens and compassionate and non-judgmental human beings. We need to raise children who are strong in mind, brave in heart and healthy in body. Resilience, knowing community and instilling a love of learning are key in the stakes of life as it is now.

This book is written for parents who know the days can seem long with our precious children, but the years are too short and soon enough our kids will be walking out the door to their life. Our job right now is to make sure we have prepared our children with the right skills to take this leap and at the same time allowed them time to enjoy their childhood. Show them love, show them how to build a solid, respectful relationship, show them how to live in the moment, create fun, happy memories, show them how to bounce back to ride the ups and downs and show them how to belong and connect.

Parenting is not meant to be easy so let's ride this journey together.

– ANNA PARTRIDGE

CHAPTER 1

What is resilience?

'Do not judge me by my successes, judge me by how many times I fell down and got back up again.'

– NELSON MANDELA

One of the key ingredients to mental wellbeing is developing and maintaining resilience: mental resilience, emotional resilience and physical resilience.

Our children need to be mentally, physically and emotionally resilient to be able to ride this wave of life. They need to have strategies to bounce back. They need to feel a sense of belonging and significance and above all they need to feel connected to their families and communities to feel a sense of wellbeing.

Building resilience is a key factor to buffering anxiety and depression because when our children know they can bounce back, they do. When they have the strategies and support around them, they can weather the storm. Children who are anxious and are diagnosed with depression bounce back when they know they are not alone and have good strategies to deal with their worries. Resilience is a key factor to building a strong mind, brave heart and healthy body.

The scientific definition of resilience is the power or ability to return to the original form or position after being bent, compressed or stretched.

When referring to resilience in us, it is about the ability to be strong, healthy or successful again after something adverse or bad has happened. The definition of resilience used here is the ability to bounce back from life's setbacks physically, emotionally and mentally.

Resilient people;
- Are brilliant at problem solving as a coping mechanism to deal with stress including taking charge of a problem
- Have the ability to face their fears and take risks
- Have lower levels of denial, avoidant coping behaviour and behaviour disengagement
- Have high positive emotional intelligence and optimism and the ability to reframe adverse experiences in a positive light
- Are socially competent and know how to ask for help
- Have a natural ability to build their own community with connected, strong friendships/relationships
- Are flexible in their thinking with attention and focus
- Have a sense of purpose and belonging
- Have a well-defined moral compass, belief system or faith to find meaning in the midst of trauma
- Can find humour in serious situations
- Know the boundaries between themselves and trauma and grief
- Have self-awareness of their environment and state (including self-confidence and self-esteem)
- Have great self-care habits including a creative outlet, exercise, community support or a regular care routine like massages, facials, and pedicures.
- Are logical and rational in the face of stress and adversity (not over catastrophes or irrational)

'At the heart of resilience is a belief in oneself – yet also a belief in something larger than oneself. Resilient people do not let adversity define them. They find resilience by moving towards a goal beyond themselves, transcending pain and grief by perceiving bad times as a temporary state of affairs.'

– HARA ESTROFF MARANO,
Editor-at-Large for Psychology Today.

So what does a resilient child look like?

A resilient child is someone who is learning and mastering the ability to bounce back from an adverse situation mentally, emotionally and physically.

Building resilience in our children is not like teaching good manners or teaching the skill of skipping or hopping. Resilience is more complex and long term. Children need to learn and develop resilience often and in many situations. We can build resilience through our words, actions and the environment we provide.

Here are some questions to determine how resilient your child is now…

- How does you child deal with disappointment?
- Does your child solve problems on their own or come to you?
- How does your child deal with falling over on the playground?
- Does your child have a strong self-image?
- Does your child eat well? Exercise enough? Get enough sleep?
- Does your child make friends easily?
- Can your child tell you when they are sad, angry, and happy and really recognize their emotions?
- Does your child love learning and love school?

Your child's ability to problem solve their own concerns, their independent nature, their physical state, their ability to deal with emotions, their self-confidence and body image and their capacity to learn all go towards determining how resilient our children already are and with any of these lacking, determine the areas we need to work with them to further build their resilience skills further.

Fig. 1 shows the successful outcome model for children who are resilient. I created this model to be used in schools and with families to demonstrate the steps a resilient child will go through when faced with a setback or adversity. It is a continuum from when the adversity or setback hits, right through to reaching a successful outcome.

For a child to reach a successful outcome or be resilient, they will draw on their own schema, past experiences and cues from adults around them to interpret the situation. They will then lean heavily on their capacity to be resilient to react to the situation. Their actions will result in either a positive or negative outcome.

The model works like this.

ADVERSITY HITS: The adversity that hits is classified into two categories. It is either a crisis which are generally sudden, unexpected and have a major impact on activities, events or situations such as death, moving, divorce, acts of violence. It can also include smaller unexpected adversity such as disappointment or something that doesn't go the child's way. Or it can be chronic, ongoing stress that can include childhood neglect, unmet needs, chronic sibling fighting or bullying at school or a bad school or home environment.

HOW DO I INTERPRET THE ADVERSITY?: The way a child interprets the adversity is based on their past experiences of such an event, activity or situation. They have built a way to see the world through their own schema and this will influence how they interpret the adversity. It will also be determined by the genetic disposition and

WHAT IS RESILIENCE?   11

Successful outcome model for children who are resilient

Adversity hits

The adversity is either a CRISIS or CHRONIC

CRISIS	CHRONIC
- death - moving house or school	- neglect - unmet needs
- physical or mental pain - divorce	- sibling fighting - bullying
- violence	- poor school environment

How do I interpret the adversity?

Many factors influence how we interpret adversity including:
- past experiences or schema - genetic disposition
- impact on me (risks involved) - location or situation
- take cues from others including peers or adults - people involved

What is my resilience capacity?

STRONG MIND	BRAVE HEART	HEALTHY BODY
- rational decision making	- capacity to build strong relationships - non-judgment with parents, siblings, wider community - empathy	- well rested ie. not tired
- problem solving skills		- physically able
strong core beliefs and values		- eaten well
- bank of positive schema	- high emotional intelligence	- high levels of energy
	- well developed social skills	

How do I react?

Enact your STRONG MIND, BRAVE HEART AND HEALTHY BODY

Successful outcome from an adverse situation

How do you know if it is successful?

In the short term, the crisis is averted, emotions are calmed and peace is restored. Help may have been accessed and routine and habits return to normal for that child's life.

In the long term, the adversity is seen as a 'low' in the pattern of life and highs in life have been achieved again.

Fig. 1   © Anna Partridge their sensed or perceived immediate risk to them. To cue this, they will assess their immediate surrounds and take cues from peers or adults. This is where our role modeling of parents is important.

WHAT IS MY RESILIENCE CAPACITY?: Their capacity for resilience will come into play strongly here. This is how strong their mind is, how brave their heart is or how healthy their body is. These will determine their level of ability to bounce back and how successful the outcome form the adverse situation will be.

If a child has a strong mind or mental resilience – they will call on their good decision making skills, problem-solving skills, and agile mind from the maximum opportunity to learn as children, their brain capacity and the core values and belief system they have already formed.

If a child has a brave heart or emotional resilience – they will have learnt how to handle a situation based on their strong relationships with an adult, with the community and with their siblings. They will be emotionally ready to deal with the stress in a more rational way without over catastrophizing. They will back their decision in with their high levels of self-confidence, non-judgmental character, independent streak and ability to empathize and be compassionate towards others.

If a child has a strong body or physical resilience – they will have the energy and grit to be able to deal with the situation long term. They will have self-care skills to nurture their body in times of stress and adversity and know how to provide it with adequate nutrition. Their genetic make up will be strong and able to withstand the stress without getting ill.

HOW DO I REACT?: They will react to a situation by enacting their strong mind, healthy body and brave heart and reach a successful and positive outcome. The stage between How do I react? and Successful Outcome will often be the longest stage and will vary on length depending on the severity of the adversity.

SUCCESSFUL OUTCOME FROM ADVERSE SITUATION: The child has bounced back or is resilient to the adversity or setback. This will look different in every situation.

Let's run this model through a scenario.

April is 9 years old. Her grandmother died overnight and this morning her mother told her she had died. The first thing she will be doing subconsciously is thinking of what death means to her. These questions might be scanning through her head – who has died that I know? Was it a sad experience? Now they are dead, what happens? Will she be in heaven or somewhere else? Who is going to make our rainbow birthday cakes now she is dead? I wonder if I can see her. Mum is pretty sad so that means I probably need to be sad too – but Dad isn't crying so maybe it is OK if I don't cry. The only person April knew that had died was one of Grandma's friends a few years ago and didn't really pay too much attention to it. All she knew was that Grandma had been a bit sad and gone to a funeral – whatever that was.

April had a great relationship with her grandmother and also has a strong relationship with her mum. She knows her mum is sad and so she is sad too. She starts crying softly and cuddles her mum. She then goes into her room and gets a photo of her grandma and tells a story about her grandma when she came to her 8th birthday party and danced to the Top 10 hit 'Shut up and Dance' when it came on. She waited for her mum's reaction and wasn't pleased when she smiled.

She hadn't had her breakfast yet and so went to the kitchen to make her cereal and asked her mum is she wanted a cup of coffee. She knew she was sad so this might make her feel better. She went and got her school uniform on because it was Wednesday and that is what she did every Wednesday morning before school, brushed her teeth and did her hair. She knew she was sad, but she was still going to school.

She didn't know whether to ask her mum to many questions about what happens to Grandma now so she waited until she got in the car to go to school and asked dad. Dad wasn't at work yet so she guessed he would stay home and help mum today and cheer her up a bit.

When she got to school, she told her best friends and her best friends mum and they were all sad because they knew her grandma. She cried again at school, but just a little bit.

As we can see, April interpreted her Grandma's death through her schema and past experiences of death and got cues on how to react from her mum. She used her empathy and compassion to make her mum smile. She followed the habits that had already been set for a Wednesday morning by eating breakfast and getting ready for school. She was able to remember her strong relationships with her grandma and relished in that. She also knew that her mum was upset so waiting to ask her dad any questions. She then drew on her strong relationships at school with her friends and her friends mum to comfort her and help her make sense of the situation.

As a parent, where can we have the biggest impact in the resilience journey?

Both at the 'interpreting the adversity' stage and by nurturing and building on your child's resilience capacity.

Children will interpret the adversity from past experience and cueing from peers and adults. By providing rich experiences, age appropriate risk taking, independence and coaching when adversity or setbacks happen, we are building up their schema to interpret a situation quickly and without over catastrophizing.

By nurturing and building a child's resilience capacity, you are ensuring they will be in the best position to 'find' the successful outcome and bounce back. By helping our children develop a strong mind (mental resilience), brave heart (emotional resilience) and healthy body (physical resilience), we are building their resilience capacity and allowing them to successfully navigate life's ups and downs.

CHAPTER 2

The building blocks of resilience

"Resilience is not just a result of biological predisposition. Developmental research has shown that parenting choices taken while the child's brain and nervous system are still developing are crucial when it comes to overcoming trauma later on."

– STEVEN SOUTHWICK,
Professor of psychiatry at the Yale School of Medicine

Understanding where our own resilience comes from helps to be able to nurture it in our children.

It is strongly argued that the ability to bounce back is innate. In the debate of nature versus nurture, we are born with resilience – some more than others. It is along the way with the experiences we are subject to and the way we are raised where it is either nurtured or it evaporates.

Think about a toddler. When a toddler is learning to walk, they are unsteady on their feet. They fall down and get up and fall down and get up. This goes on for about two or three months until eventually they start running. Even after a year of walking, they are still not completely stable and they fall over and run and fall over and run again.

Earlier on when a child was learning to crawl or even roll over, the same thing happened. They tried and tried and tried until they eventually succeeded. Children are inbuilt with resilience. They know at this point it is important to bounce back. They know if they keep on trying, they will eventually walk. I have an image in my mind of my little boy getting so frustrated with learning to crawl that he would rock on his knees and start crying out of sheer frustration of not being able to move. The next day he would get up and try again. And when he did actually crawl, at 8 months old he had the biggest, cutest grin on his face you could imagine. He had succeeded.

Even at this very young age, I encouraged my son. I told him he could do it. When he fell over and cried out of frustration, I cuddled him. I got down on my hands and knees and crawled with him. So did my 2-year-old daughter and so did my husband. My father in law even joined in. It must have looked pretty funny seeing us through the window – the four of us crawling around the house with my son trying to follow. And then when my boy could stand, he was over the moon about it and started to fall down, get up, fall down, get up all over again.

It is right from this very early age we can nurture resilience in our children.

The scenario of being able to crawl for my son could have been very different. If he cried out of sheer frustration to crawl and I picked him up every time, he would not have been encouraged him to crawl. If I had been ambivalent about him crawling in the first place and not encouraging, maybe he would have known it wasn't important to start moving. These little gestures help our kid's pick up on our excitement, encouragement and sense of nurture from a very early age.

Some children are born with more resilience than others.

A study lead by the Durham Child Health and Development Study Center looked at how well babies regulated themselves when separated from their mothers at 3 months, 6 months and 12 months. They recorded the babies' heart rate when the mother left the room and studied the genes that regulate dopamine in the brain.

The study looked at the two types of the dopamine gene (DRD2) and its effect on resilience. The risky version of the gene is associated with impulse control disorders, aggression, ADHD, substance abuse problems and an overall lower ability to handle a situation.

The researchers found the babies who had the risky version of the dopamine gene showed less regulation when their mother left the room and their heart rate increased. This was true at 3, 6 and 12 months.

This study affirms that certain children who have lower resilience are at a higher risk of developing anxiety and stress to life's setbacks or adversities than others. It also tells us that our parenting style is key to nurturing a child's resilience.

Resilience through the ages

It is no surprise that as the years go by in childhood, exposure to stress increases and resilience is tested. Resilience or our ability to bounce back is also tested.

2-3 years old. By the age of two to three years, children are already interacting with the world and its noticeable ups and downs. They need to learn to problem solve, develop empathy, love and build healthy relationships with those around them at this age. They really start to communicate their needs and wants and we can encourage and nurture at this stage.

Children's basic needs are food, water and shelter to survive, but to thrive they need love, trust, hope and autonomy to overcome adverse situations. They need to learn how to foster relationships with caregivers. They need to learn self-confidence, emotional intelligence and have a good start to life to be resilient.

At this age, resilience is often marred by the developmental stage of being egocentric and a heavy reliance on the underdeveloped rational part of the brain. It seems their natural bent for resilience has ebbed and so, when they are learning to navigate emotions, they can play out in forms of tantrums, hitting, biting, not sharing and other physical acts. It is at this age that we help them understand and recognize emotions and start building emotional intelligence. Modeling, demonstrating and explicitly teaching what emotions look like is important at this age.

A recent study shows that boys develop their empathy by sitting on their mother's knee as a one or two year old. They learn how to understand and relate to others and build relationships by this mere act of love at this very tender age. By learning empathy, boys are able to navigate the testosterone filled teenage years and be good dads themselves. This lack of empathy building at this age is contributing to one of the reasons our boys aged 17 to 19 are among some of the most violent people in the country.

Being loved and nurtured allows children to set up healthy relationships. We are providing tools early on to help them recognize unstable relationships or tools to be able to rebuild these same relationships.

A huge change in society for this age group over the past two to three decades has been their increased attendance at daycare or preschool at 2 or 3 years old. As the primary care giver, usually the mother goes back to work and children of this age are no longer at home being explicitly taught but learning 'on the job' with other children. Choosing a childcare centre or preschool for your child that nurtures emotional and social learning is important.

Another trait with children between the ages of two and three is that they are little sponges. They want to explore the world – touch, taste, hear and smell everything, taking everything in and making sense of the world around them.

A parent I worked with had very strict rules around letting her kids into the kitchen; scared they might burn themselves on the oven or get scalded by the hot water. Or worse still she might drop a knife or hot pot onto them. They had to stop at the door or the line she marked and couldn't go past it. However, if that were the rule in our house, I would have barely seen my kids in the early days. I felt like I was constantly in the kitchen preparing the next meal. Many of our happiest times happened in the kitchen. I remember my daughter learning to roll at four months old right into the fridge. The kids would sit and eat cheerios from the cupboard. They would play in the Tupperware draw more than with their own toys and yes, they did jam their fingers in the draw when exploring, but they recovered. My daughter would sit on the bench when I was making dinner or a cake and she learnt how to measure, about textures, different sounds and colours of food. She cracked an egg at 18 months old into the cake mix and yes, the shell did go in. As she got older, she would drag the kid's table into the kitchen and play with play dough with the utensils from the kitchen cupboard for hours. My son had a dedicated lego bench to sit on in the kitchen so his little sister couldn't get to his lego and so he could talk to me while I was in the kitchen. The kitchen was the start of our place to explore the world together.

Naturally, when kids start to explore, they will put themselves at risk. Sometimes small, sometimes bigger but it is this exploring and supported risk taking that helps children build resilience. They explore their surrounds and learn how to interact with it and others.

One of the biggest challenges parents face here, is how much risk do we let our children take. There is a fine line between too much risk resulting in danger and just enough risk to allow for resilience building.

Look back to when you were a child.

Were you given some independence and freedom? Were you allowed to problem solve situations? Did you have a good relationship with your parents/siblings? Was the situation around you calm and rational or irrational and a little crazy? What challenges and stresses were you faced with and how were you supported and nurtured to deal with them?

Research strongly shows it is our childhood and upbringing that has a direct impact on how resilient we are as adults. This is why, as a parent, we have a great responsibility to build resilience in our children right from the start.

SCHOOL AGED CHILDREN. Due to safety concerns, pedophilia and child abduction, it is rare to see 9 year olds walking to the corner store or riding their bike to the park by themselves. My Mum, now in her 70s, tells of the time when she was 9 years old and one of Australia's largest cities, Sydney. She would catch a bus from her house to the train station at 7am, then a train to school for 10 stops, get off and walk a couple of blocks to school – all by herself. She was deemed old enough and society was gentle enough to let this happen.

In my own childhood we grew up on a farm in the country and were possibly given too much freedom. We would often leave the house early to go on bush walks; horse rides or on the motorbikes at ages eight, six and four for hours at a time. We experienced the ups and downs of life in those few hours and didn't have our parents to tell us not to jump the riverbank on our motorbikes or not to climb the tree that was in the back paddock. We were trusted to be OK and we were.

I remember we had a chicken shed. When I was three years old, we had 30 chooks and this one morning it was time to clip their wings to stop them flying out. I had done it before and they flap around and fly over your head and I didn't particularly want to help clip their wings with my mum and two brothers that day. So I waited outside the 6-foot high metal gate with the egg bucket. The chook shed didn't face the gate so I couldn't see my mum and brothers, but they were only about

4 metres from me. While I was waiting, a 6-foot brown snake came out of the boards right next to me and slithered into my egg bucket. Instinct must have kicked in and I knew what to do. I was so scared so I got to higher ground. I had the sense to scale the six feet tall metal wire gate and sat perched on top of a thin, metal wire, calling to my mum. My mum and brothers came running out of the chook shed and saw the big snake slithering away. Mum, Dad and the boys searched for the snake for hours after that and I think eventually they gave up. I felt safe and protected and sure mum was relieved I knew what to do, even though they were not with me at the time because this is the sort of house we grew up in.

Would this scenario happen today? Probably not. I can't imagine my own children being left long enough, or out of sight of their parents for the length of time it takes for a snake to slither out of the boards and into an egg bucket. The tendency now is to keep our children within sight and to protect them from every hazard that MIGHT happen. It is these encounters that help our kids problem solve, gain responsibility and encounter risk. I am not suggesting we leave our kids in the path of a snake however, I am suggesting we provide them with independence and age appropriate risk to experience setbacks, challenges and to solve problems.

I know society has changed with risk and the perception of risk, and I am probably at times as guilty as the next mother for over protecting my kids, however there are certain things children should be allowed to do on their own. When my two older children were 10 and 8 they would often wait for my after school outside the school gate. Their school was in a densely populated, upper class suburb in Sydney and it was difficult to find a parking spot as I rushed from work to collect them. The bell would ring at 3pm and if I couldn't get a park, I would drive around the block a few times until I could, past my kids each time I went around. Sometimes they were still waiting at the gate on the second or third lap (two or three minutes), as there was still no parking space available and so I would call out to them from the car window to say 'I am just doing another lap' and they were fine with it. There were 400 kids at the school and many parents coming in and out. This one day, I was doing my third lap and it was 3.04pm. I had seen my children twice between 3pm and 3.04pm but still couldn't get a park. My phone rang and when I answered on the car phone, it was another mum from the school calling to tell me how wrong it was for me to leave my kids at the front gate – for 4 minutes! Little did she know I had seen them twice in this period of time. This school is in one of the safest suburbs in the city and I had calculated the risk and deemed it to be fine to leave the kids at the gate with 400 kids and their parents coming out.

Sadly, the news I had left my kids standing at the gate spread like wildfire through the mum fraternity that I was a 'bad mum' and subsequent play dates were cancelled for the next afternoon. I didn't tell them that we live near one of the 'most dangerous' suburbs in Sydney and I have walked my kids down the main strip of Kings Cross! Through this act of 'disobedience' of leaving my kids at the gate, I was actually giving my children some sense of independence and responsibility. They were experiencing four minutes of freedom (with other children and parents) at the gate in a safe environment. It was helping them develop their sense of self-knowledge and I trusted them to be sensible. It had a much higher order of thinking than knowing they might be standing outside the school gates by themselves.

I couldn't help to think back to when I was at school 30 years earlier and at aged five and I walked with my eight year old brother at least six blocks from school to my mum's work every afternoon. My brother and I were fine. We actually loved it and Mum knew we were safe to be walking this way. Sometimes we even took the risk of walking through the supermarket car park instead of on the footpath, and we were equally fine and sometimes we stopped to buy a couple of lolly bags and even then, we were fine. Since the school gate incident, we live in an even safer city and my youngest daughter who is now 10 catches the tram home with her friend and walks to either her house or our house, all by themselves. Sometimes they drop into McDonald's and buy sundaes and chips and they love it. Thankfully there are no parents at this school judging my decision to allow my child to have some independence.

Resilience comes from allowing our children to problem solve, taking age appropriate risks, teaching and coaching self-esteem and self-confidence. It also comes from building a mutually respectfully relationship where a child knows you trust and respect them.

If resilience is being able to bounce back, we must let our children take risks. Risks at this age are about exploring their natural surrounds, both inside and out. To children, the risks could be as simple as dipping their toes into a puddle or jumping over a stick in the back garden or even riding a scooter ahead of their parents. When they are a bit older, it might be letting them walk to the corner store to get an ice cream on their own or sending them into the service station to buy milk while you sit in the car. These may sound small for us, but they are about exploring and building independence for our children.

Kids need to climb trees. It's one of those risks where the good far outweighs the bad. At five, one of my daughter's was a wonderful climber. She used to amaze everyone at preschool as she deftly climbed to the top of the tree in the yard and her balance was brilliant. She was just born a natural climber. At 13 months, I came into the kitchen and my daughter was standing on the kitchen bench. I scolded my husband for putting her up there but alas he didn't. We took her down and she climbed back up by curling her toes around the knobs on the drawers. So I let her climb (not on the kitchen bench however!). She is now a great gymnast and is really flexible in her upper body. Heights don't worry her and while she has fallen out of the tree a few time and scratched her leg on the bark, but she still wants to climb the tree.

From climbing trees, my daughter has learnt how to be nimble on branches, navigated the next branch to get in and out of the tree, tested to see which branch she should hold onto or step on to, seen the world from the upper branches of a tree and problem solved to get up and down in the best/quickest/most fun/safest way. And she has bounced back from her scratches and falls and is still OK about climbing trees.

As our children grow, we need to support their quest for resilience. When children are 8 or 9, they are interacting with the world to develop their sense of right and wrong and moderate their internal judgment system. At this age, as parents, we need to encourage them to work out how to overcome the wrongs and know what feels right to them.

We need to build their emotional intelligence and be good role models for them when bouncing back ourselves. This is not always easy and often we need to dig deep. We need to find our own fight to bounce back, not over catastrophize situations and not let fear hold us back. We need to show our children we have the ability to be bent and stretched and still wake up the next day and move our feet. We need to build a solid relationship so they have our support to navigate the world, however we need to find the line of supporting and smothering.

12-13 YEARS. By the time our children reach 12 to 13 years of age, we have either done our job of building resilience or not. This is the age they have gained their independence and their decision-making skills are honed. They are making decisions on a daily basis without our help and having to navigate the tough world of high school – the friendships and relationships, the workload and puberty. They are moving from childhood to adulthood. We are no longer there to hold their hand or whisper words of encouragement. We are now a sounding board for them. Nurturing our relationships with our children takes a front seat and we still will be talking through emotions and problem solving, but by now they are using much of what we have taught them in the past 12 or 13 years to navigate the ups and downs of life on their own.

With this in mind, 12 or 13 years is not a long time to build this thing called resilience. So, what can you do to give your children the best chance to navigate the ups and downs of life successfully and with a positive outcome? Build mental, emotional and physical resilience early and often.

> '*More than education, more than experience, more than training, a person's level of resilience will determine who succeeds and who fails. That's true in the cancer ward, its true in the Olympics, and it's true in the boardroom*'.
>
> DEAN BECKER,
> Harvard Business Review, May 2002

PART 1

Building a Strong Mind
(Mental Resilience)

WHAT IS MENTAL RESILIENCE?

If resilience is the capacity to face, overcome and be strengthened by the adversities of life, for our children to be resilient they need to learn how to overcome these adversities with logical, well-informed thought processes and a toolbox of knowledge to help achieve the best outcome to the adversity or setback. This 'toolbox' comes in the form of a strong mind or 'mental resilience'.

Generally, our first reaction to an adverse situation is emotional or irrational. However, a mentally resilient person has the ability to react rationally, with problem solving skills and logical thought. This mindset can only be achieved if we teach our children the tools they need to be mentally resilient.

A person who is mentally resilient;

- Makes good, informed decisions;
- Has skills and tools in place to bounce back from adverse situations;
- Is confident with high self esteem;
- Mitigates the risk of adversity through well planned life decisions and making good choices;
- Has a well-developed schema with a solid base of great memories.
- Has a strong values and beliefs system in place with the ability to make good choices and life decision;
- Has an inquiring mind with good problem solving skills; and
- Has a positive, optimistic outlook on life.

In addition to this mindset, a mentally resilient person can also potentially mitigate the risk of adversity by making sustainable life decisions and good choices throughout life. While we can't always control the ups and downs we experience, there is control over such factors as income, job status, housing and general living standards. The idea here is to provide our children with a solid mental base and a strong mind so they can reduce the controllable lows of life. These children also know that they can control their thoughts. These thoughts have an impact on their feelings and then actions. The power of knowledge to control thought is important in the building block of resilience.

As an adult if you are in the position to have a stable income, live with a roof over your head and can pay the bills, you will reduce the risk of becoming homeless. If you have had a good education or have gained a trade, you will ideally have more chance of getting a stable job and income. If you are focused, motivated and have high self-esteem, you are probably more likely to seek new opportunities in life. If you can change your negative thoughts to positive thoughts and then create a positive feeling rather than a negative one, this will affect the choices you make in life.

How can we ensure our children are mentally resilient? This is what is covered in Part 1.

1. Provide a positive learning environment at home
2. Give children a good start to life. Much of our brain's capacity is developed in the first five years of life and this patterning will remain with a child for the rest of their lives.
3. Provide a good education
4. Develop a strong values and beliefs system
5. Build up a bank of positive memories
6. Encourage a growth mindset with a positive outlook on life
7. Build self-esteem and self-confidence
8. Facilitate an understanding of financial matters

CHAPTER 3

Provide a positive learning environment at home

Our children are born little sponges. They are wired to soak up the world around them and learn. As young as three months, babies are taking in what they hear, see, feel, touch and taste, maybe even younger. As toddlers, this thirst for knowledge and curiosity is ever ripe and continues to develop as they grow into school children. Our job as parents is to nurture this curiosity, thirst for knowledge and help our children develop a 'strong mind' right from the start.

If you have a 4-year-old it may not surprise you to know they ask 394 questions a day – that is close to 105,000 questions a year! At this age, children are desperately trying to make sense of the world around them. To build a strong mind, the way we respond to these questions has the ability to nurture a child's curiosity, develop an inquiring mind, a problem solver and life long learner.

By age nine, a child only asks 169 questions each day. Is this because they have made more sense of their world? Or is it because they have sadly been discouraged from asking questions and being curious about the world?

To set our children on this path to mental resilience, we need to provide them with a rich, positive learning environment at home, feed their curiosity and challenge them with questions and seek answers.

As parents, we are our children's first teachers, so it is important to set up a positive learning environment for our children at home to allow them to interact with the world and make sense of it. By doing this, you are creating an early love of learning and wonder and the best opportunity to learn.

CREATE A SPACE FOR LEARNING IN YOUR HOME

From the age of about one or two-years-old, create a space somewhere in your home where your children can learn and explore. This space is not necessarily in a formal setting, but in a play based setting.

If you are lucky enough to have a playroom, make it engaging and fill it with art work from your children, a book shelf, age appropriate toys, colourful pictures invoking curiosity, letters, numbers and colours. As they get older put timetables up, sight words, a world map, their own master art works or the writing they bring home from preschool or school.

A friend of mine has a toy room and every couple of weeks, she allows her girls to redesign it. At age 4 and 9, they take full responsibility for this room and set it up the way they want it. Right now it has a kitchen area with the pretend oven, a 'lounge room' for reading books, a make shift shed to keep tools and 'things' in and a writing wall to put their stories up. It is welcoming, safe and warm room to walk into and a great idea to designate the responsibility of a space to the girls. They are more careful to clean it up after using it and take pride in a space that is theirs. They can also create in there and make their own adventures.

If you don't have a playroom, make part of the lounge room into a learning space. Bedrooms don't work as well as they are not frequented enough by the whole family to see and create conversation about the work or creativity that is going on in this space and ideas in the space are easily forgotten.

Some other ideas for your learning space may include:

- A discovery table (more in the curiosity section)
- A creation table
- A tub full of pencils, paper, pens, textas, glue, paint and paint brushes
- Musical instruments
- Book shelf and reading corner
- There might be a toy library near by to swap toys every few weeks
- Somewhere to pack every thing away at the end of the day, like a toy cupboard or shelves or one of IKEA's many storage ideas.

The key to making this space work is spending spend time with your child in their learning space or making it so close to the kitchen so you can make meals while they are creating.

Have toys: but don't go overboard

> *"The potential possibilities of any child are the most intriguing and stimulating in all creation."*
>
> – Ray L. Wilbur

Children do not need lots of toys. They need a few good quality, age appropriate toys to stimulate their love of learning, curiosity, creativity and sense of wonder.

At a family Christmas a few years ago when my niece was 11 months old, she had been laden with blocks and dollies and books and loud, light up toys that moved. After she had opened her presents, she sat in the cardboard box that the presents came in playing with the wrapping paper for hours without looking back at the toys.

Even the Tupperware draw in the kitchen is a source of huge entertainment. Who knew there was so much fun to be had by putting plastic containers inside each other one after one or building block towers at the age of 13 months with plastic containers?

Here's some reasons why giving children fewer toys is a good idea;

- Kids learn to be more creative and resourceful with what they have
- Kids develop a longer attention span and focus on one object because they are content with the thing they are playing with rather than looking for more
- Kids learn to take greater care of the things they have
- There is less expectation for material goods to entertain them so they seek more creative avenues.

IDEAS FOR 'AGE APPROPRIATE' TOYS TO STIMULATE CURIOSITY, CREATIVITY AND A LOVE OF LEARNING

0-12 MONTHS
- An exersaucer
- Play frame
- Soft toys with parts that can be sucked, chewed and crinkled
- Board books
- Soft material books
- Soft balls to roll
- Stacking blocks

1-2 YEARS
- Stacking Blocks
- Wooden blocks
- Paints and paint brushes
- Balls
- Baby dolls and stuffed toys
- Board books
- Soft material books
- Play dough

2-5 YEARS
- Dress up box
- Well stocked craft box
- Duplo/Lego
- Figurines
- Farm animals
- Train track
- Car track or garage
- Toy cars and trains
- Balls and bats
- Dolls
- Puzzles
- Magna Doodle (magnetic drawing board)

5-12 YEARS
- Lego
- Remote control car or helicopter
- Slot car racing track
- Cricket set
- Netball or basket ball hoop and ball
- Skipping rope
- Dolls or Action figures to create scenes

- Trampoline
- Sketch a graph
- Art supplies (paint, paper, metallic pencils, cardboard, marker pens, textas, glue, scissors, pipe cleaners).

READ TO YOUR KIDS EVERYDAY AND ALWAYS

If you read to your child for just 10 minutes a day as a baby, they are six times more likely to read as adults. Being able to read well positively affects every subject at school and allows children to explore a new world of opportunity and adventure.

It is never too early to start reading to your child, even in the womb. It may seem a little strange to read to your tummy, however a baby develops the ability to hear sounds at about 18 weeks gestation. Babies develop ears at eight weeks gestation but it takes another three months before they can actually pick up sound. The first sound a baby hears is the beat of their mother's heartbeat and then they will start to hear noises from the environment such as music, television, your voice and other family members.

If you read to your baby after it is born, they will recognize your voice and it will be soothing for them. This is also the perfect time to make up stories during the day and even start to add reading to the daily routine. For example, at night you might bath your baby, read it a story, feed it and put it to bed. Robyn Baker, author of Baby Love is a big advocate of starting as you mean to go on and ten years after my first child was born, I still keep a similar routine to bath, dinner, read story, bed. At this early stage of your new baby there is no need for lots of books – just a couple of board books are great.

Once your child is one or two-years-old, it is time to start filling the bookshelf. Maybe from your own childhood you will remember a bookshelf or space where you had your own books or toys and you can build the same in your child's room or in the living area (or playroom if you have one). Ideally your book area is in a quieter space, preferably a different room to your television. Providing a comfortable, inviting space around the book area is also good – maybe with a few cushions or a couch. Some of the fondest memories of my son, who is now eight years old, are of him sitting next to the kid's bookshelf in the playroom at 16 months carefully pulling every book off the shelf and going through each page before moving on to the next book. He would do this for hours. My son is now my most avid reader and has a super imagination.

Don't restrict reading to just books – make it a part of everything children are doing. Here are some examples:

- Every technological device and even the television have text that a child needs to read.
- Help your child read the instructions for games.
- New toys generally come in a box with instructions or promotional material to read. Read the cereal box in the morning.
- Read signs on the side of the road on the way to school in the morning.
- Read the headlines of the newspaper together.
- Read the safety instructions at the pool or the safety card on the plane.
- Read the front of the mail out of the mailbox with your child.

The list is endless.... there are so many words all around us and it is essential to get our kids to understand reading is not just important for books but for navigating our way around, performing tasks and interacting with the world.

When your child starts reading, it is the most wonderful thing to watch. All of a sudden, they see words that actually have a meaning for the first time and can make sense of them. Foster this achievement. One of the biggest elements of a beginning reader is confidence. If you correct every second word or belittle their effort – they will struggle to read as quickly. Don't make it a chore. Set up a good routine early on with those little home readers and read it together before bed or before dinner. If it becomes a struggle, leave it for a week and come back to it.

Encourage children to read books they like. If they are reading 'Nip and Fluff' as a home reader and hate it, change it up with reading a book about dinosaurs, science experiments, the Guinness Book of Records or whatever they are passionate about at the time. Or read an eBook on their iPad or computer together.

If your child sees you reading, they will also be encouraged to read. How often do you sit down and pick up a book, magazine or newspaper? The more we can model how to be a good reader to our children, the quicker they associate it with something important for them to do.

Value your child's work

I was teaching a Year 2 class the other day and the children had to choose five spelling words and write a sentence with each one. One little girl chose 'rubbish' and this was her sentence – 'I took my art work home yesterday and mum said it was rubbish'. It was a true sentence and she had spent many lessons on this piece of work for it to go into the bin.

These little things matter to our children. Value what they are proud of and stick it up around the house or put it over the playroom walls. If you don't have a playroom, make a part of the lounge room for the kids work and display it proudly (not all of it as it may take up three rooms, but the most important pieces). Right now, we have a kitchen wall full of paintings. Put their writing up. Display their homemade books on the bookshelf. Keep their best artwork in a box so they can see it later. Put their Easter egg creations up (for a little while) or their Christmas decorations onto the tree.

Play games with your kids

Think back to when you were a child. What were your favourite games to play? Did you play it as a family, on your own or with your siblings? I distinctly remember playing card games like cheat, poker and rummy with my Granny and Grandpa. I also remember playing Monopoly and Trouble with my brothers and family friends. Our friends had the Hungry Hippo game and Mouse Trap and I couldn't wait to go to their house to play it with them. Playing games like elastics, marbles and What's the Time Mr Wolf were also high on the game agenda.

There are so many great reasons to play games with your child.

Let's look at a classic game, Snakes and Ladders. There are between 2 to 4 players in the game so each child needs to wait their turn. They roll a dice (or two) and need to count on or add up. There are consequences for their actions – if they land of a snake, they go back and if they land on a ladder, they go forward. If you have listened to your kids play snakes and ladders, they are talking all the time about the game so it is promoting language, vocabulary and focus. If you lose, you deal with disappointment and if you win, you learn how to be respectful and not boast. Playing this, or one of the many variations of the game now, with an adult signal to kids that they matter and you are on their level.

Why are games so important for kids?
- They encourage our kids to make choices about their move or which cards they will put down when
- There are often consequences for their actions
- There is a winner and a looser helping our children deal with both disappointment and boasting
- Children learn the necessary skills to work together as a team
- Maths skills can be involved. Either basic skills like counting forwards or backwards or tallying to more complex skills such as

working with money like in Monopoly or evaluating probabilities.
- Literacy skills can be involved. Scrabble is a classic example of this.
- Games promote problem solving skills and the ability to think ahead
- Playing a game together as a family gives everyone a single focus and the opportunity to be engaged in something together.

10 Classic Board Games to play with Kids
- Monopoly
- Scrabble
- Trouble
- Connect 4
- Chess
- Snakes and Ladders
- Chinese Checkers
- Twister
- Candy Land
- Guess Who

10 Card Games to play with Kids
- Uno
- Rummy
- Poker
- Old Maid
- Memory match
- Snap
- Pairs
- Go Fish
- Charades
- Crazy 8s

6 Online Games to play with Kids

(online games work to promote all the skills like a board or card game if they are two or more player and they can take turns with someone else. There are also some great online apps for two of more players).

- ABC 3 games ABC 3 (http://www.abc.net.au/abc3/games/)
- PBS Kids games (http://pbskids.org/games/)
- Nick games (http://www.nick.com/games/multiplayer-games/)
- Cool maths games (http://www.coolmath-games.com)
- Nick Jr games (http://www.nickjr.com/games/)
- Girls go games (http://www.girlsgogames.com)

10 Outdoor Games to do with Kids

- Hopscotch
- Elastics or skipping (jump rope)
- Marbles
- Ball games – cricket, football, netball, baseball
- What's the Time Mr Wolf
- Hide and Seek
- Jacks
- Red light, Green light
- Marco Polo
- Flying a kite

Foster your child's imagination and creativity

In our 'hurry up' culture where everything is moving at a million miles an hour, every hour in our child's day is accounted for. At school, there is a jam-packed curriculum that must be met each day and when our kids get home, they are ferried off to the next after school activity or play date. With a packed schedule, it is leaving little time for our children to be creative and imaginative.

This goes against a child's natural tendency to use their vivid imagination or leap into a creative project. If we don't nurture it, it sadly slowly dwindles away. Having this curiosity and imagination is vital for a strong mind and helps to be able to solve problems to bounce back from adversity. People who are mentally resilient can think outside the square and find the best outcome from their adverse situation. If we limit this capacity, we are doing our children a disservice in the longer term.

By nurturing creativity and imagination, it will help our children develop social skills, decision making skills, confidence, self expression and independence which all add to mental resilience. It can also provide our children with a place to escape from the everyday pressures of rules, regulations and the fast pace lifestyles we now lead.

By the age of two or three-years-old, our child's imagination really starts to fire up. If you spend time in a preschool classroom or even in your own house with kids this age, you will know the magic that can be created from a plain, old cardboard box. Kids really can create life from anything. They can put toilet paper rolls on a box to make arms, dangling bits of string for legs and poking sticks in for eyes this box is now 'real' and often even gets given a name and a voice. The same could happen if you give them an old sock – they will come back with it turned into a snake or other wriggling, 'live' creature with eyes, mouth and nose. We moved recently and my children spent hours playing 'guinea pigs' in the many cardboard boxes. They created a whole imaginary guinea pig world complete with guinea pig houses and had guinea pig names like Furry Pig and Fluffy. It even had ramps to go up and down and beds to sleep in. It was beautiful to listen to.

Children's dreams also become more vivid at this age. If they can remember a dream when they wake up, it is often a mixed up journey and very colourful. Imaginary friends may also start to pop up. At 3, my son had an imaginary friend called Dolly who would meet us in a certain tree that we had to visit every day. He would make up stories of adventures Dolly had been on and it was priceless listening to them.

If we allow our children to create and nurture it, it can be amazing. My nephew was living in the hills in India when he was four years old. Being a very creative family, my brother in law put up an old double sized bed sheet on the wall and gave his son paints and pencils. He created the most elaborate scene complete with mountains, rivers, houses, trees and even the people he had met in India. It a beautiful mix of with what he saw outside his home with his own imagination and fantasy, from the level of a 4 year old. It was a true masterpiece. However, it doesn't have to be that elaborate. A piece of paper with pencils and time to create allows children the freedom to use their imagination and creativity that is flowing in massive proportions at this age.

10 WAYS TO FOSTER YOUR CHILD'S IMAGINATION AND CREATIVITY

CREATE AN IMAGINATION TUB. Find an old tub or box and put paint, pencils, buttons, sticks, boxes, glue, paper, play dough – anything you can find around the house that you don't use anymore. This will be your kids 'go to' box to create. They can use their creative freedom to imagine and make whatever they like. If your child is more into building, this tub could have toys that allow children to use their imagination when playing such as Lego, plain blocks, figurines, cars or trains and train tracks.

LET YOUR KIDS BE BORED. While it has become part of the norm, we don't actually need to fill up every bit of spare time for our kids with after school activities, planned sport or planned trips to the zoo.

Our kids need time to be bored so they can use their imagination and creativity to make up games or design tunnels out of blankets and pillows in the lounge room or to go outside and make a fairy garden out of old sticks and pebbles. When your kids say they are bored, don't fill in the void. Let them go off and see what happens next – it might just be awesome.

MESS IS GOOD! Who's afraid of letting their kids paint in the house?? If you said yes, I'm buying you a paint box, some plastic to put under the table and some courage! Often the best creations come out of mess! If we teach our kids how to clean up and set the expectations around them cleaning up after themselves – mess is gone in no time at all. AND think of the fun the kids have had making that mess to get to their creation. Mess = creativity and imagination.

TURN OFF THE TELEVISION AND COMPUTER GAMES. Children have their own world of imagination in their heads – once they are spending all their time in a new imaginary world on a computer or on the television, it takes over their natural world. When I taught a Year 1 class, I taught an activity where children had to write a story titled 'The night my toy came alive'. One boy could only write about the scene from Avengers and Skylanders. There was no original thought. It was as though his own imagination had been taken over by the fantasy on TV and in his video games. I spoke to his parents and they said he spent the majority of his time watching or playing his X-Box Avenger and Sky Landers games and because he was so into it, they bought him books to go with it. AND then they had bought him the toys to go with it. So for the past year, he had been creating these scenes directly from the movies, books or X-Box and couldn't think outside it. His parents slowly eased off on the technology, books and toys and replaced it with going outside, having fun together and chapter books. By the end of the year there was a marked improvement in his imagination.

LIMIT COLOURING IN. When my daughter started Kindergarten she had a vivid, beautiful imagination. Her teachers idea of art was to give the children cut out pieces of paper to make a tiger or a Christmas tree. There was no avenue to create. And colouring in became the busy time activity. When she finished her work, she would colour in. It took about 6 months for her to loose her creative flair and when she came home, she no longer wanted to paint and draw her amazing pictures. She had been channeled into limited creativity and colouring in and confined by lines and boxes. It was so sad. Giving a child a blank piece of paper with some scaffolding and some paints, textas and pencils to create gives them freedom of expression and again opens up the channels of creating and imagining.

SPEND TIME OUTSIDE PLAYING. Nature has the best toys! With sticks, leaves, grass, muddy puddles and pebbles – kids can create the most intricate, imaginary worlds for fairies and other creatures to be a part of. Sometimes on the playground, and even with my own kids, I sit and listen to the amazing games the kids can get into just by building their worlds from nature. Nature also has trees to climb and caves to explore that spark imagination.

TELL MADE UP STORIES. One of the best ways to spark imagination is to tell children made up stories – not from a book, but just out of our heads. My husband has created a whole world with my kids using a character Bertie the Beetle. This beetle goes on great adventures through different lands and there are now many characters they meet along the way. My kid's love to add to the stories and they create this imaginary world together.

ALLOW TIME FOR CREATING. It can take time for a child to create something… have down time in your week and on your weekend where you can just be at home and get out the Imagination Tub or go for a walk through the forest with no place to be or send your kids outside to just explore and find their own imagination and creativity right there. It is easy to schedule in play dates, after school activities each day and let kids go on technology, however some quiet time at home equals time to create and imagine.

HAVE THE WORLD'S BEST DRESS UP BOX. Dress ups are all about creating imaginary scenes and places. It doesn't need to be expensive fancy dress – it can be from your cupboard or a cape made from an old sheet or piece of material. Sheets and material can be turned into so many different creatures…your child will tell you!

BLOW BUBBLES. There is nothing more magical than a sky filled with bubbles and little children running around after them. Bubbles themselves create imagination for our children and get them outside to be in the fresh air and playing.

NURTURE YOUR CHILD'S CURIOSITY

Babies are born learners. They have a natural curiosity to figure out how the world works and want to explore with all their senses. How many times did your child at the age of 6 months pick up a toy or something from the floor and put it straight into their mouth? By nurturing their curiosity between the age of zero and five years and beyond we can harness their potential to become life long learners.

Not a day went by when my 90-year-old Grandma didn't learn something. She would tell me that the most important thing about life is to learn and never stop learning. We expand our minds, see the counter argument to long held views and have an infinite amount of knowledge and ultimately wisdom. We are hard wired to be curious and we must encourage our kids to keep asking questions and finding out about the way the world works.

Did you know that a four year old asks 387 questions every day?

Imagine for a minute if we tell our 4 year old, 'I don't have time' or I'm too busy for your silly questions' or 'Stop asking me questions all the time'. Right in those statements, we are sending the message that questioning is not a good thing and slowly stopping our child's wonder and ability to question life. We need to keep our kids asking those why questions and provide the right environment for wonder. This will encourage our children to question and find a solution to the adversities they face and allow them to bounce back more easily from a setback.

The exciting thing now that is different to when we grew up is GOOGLE. When we were kids if we asked why the sky was blue we only had a few options – the library, the encyclopedia if we were lucky enough to have the set at home or rely on the knowledge and schema from our own parents. Now, if we don't know an answer, we can Google it for our own children.

Google is also priceless in a classroom and brings immediacy to learning. When I teach primary school kids, sometimes a whole lesson is taken over by one simple question a child has asked. On Remembrance Day last year, a child asked why we were wearing red poppies – this sparked an entire 6-week exploration into the war with guest speakers, artifacts from the war and ways we can remember the people who have bravely fought for our country. This was all able to tie back into the history curriculum.

Now, more than anytime before in our parenting history, we have the necessary resources to harness our children's curiosity immediately.

5 ways to harness your child's curiosity and keep them asking questions

EXPLORE NATURE. Go on nature walks together and talk about the trees, the nuts, the sounds, the smells, ask your own questions about the sky, the half moon, the brightness of the sun.

CREATE AN EXPLORATION TABLE OR CORNER. Encourage your child to use a microscope on the table, bring in sticks or stones or shells or what ever you have found on your nature walk and find some questions to Google. This might double up as your craft table with paint, glue, play dough and cardboard boxes. If they are too young for this, provide a stimulating environment for your little ones with pictures on the walls, different textures to hold and things that make noise like squeaky toys.

ASK OPEN-ENDED QUESTIONS. These questions don't have a yes or no answer but require your child to think about and question you have just asked them. They could respond with more questions and the conversation continues. For example, instead of asking 'How was school today?', ask 'What did you do in Math today?' or 'What did you write about today?'. You can even use this as a question in response to one of their curiosity questions to further simulate their thinking.

CREATE TIME TO EXPLORE. Our children are largely overscheduled. It is a big day at school and then they do a couple of after school activities a week, have a few play dates, do their homework and there is no time left to explore and create. Have down time so your child can create and explore.

HARNESS THEIR INTERESTS. Children will naturally go through phases of exploration. It might be dinosaurs or bugs or spiders – whatever it is, provide as many learning opportunities as you can around their interest. It might be grabbing a teachable moment at the local park when you see a spider and talking about what type it is, how amazing its web is or how many legs it has.

CHAPTER 4

Give your child the best start
EARLY

The importance of the early years is now well-recognized around the world as setting the foundations for learning, development and much of the emotional intelligence that happens with our kids.

The experiences and the relationships parents build with their children between the ages of 0 and 5 years has a long-term effect affect on the social and emotional wellbeing of our children and their mental resilience.

Brain development, development of speech and language and finding the best care options for young children are all major considerations for building a strong mind from zero to five.

BRAIN DEVELOPMENT

Zero to five year, or before a child enters formal schooling is the crucial time for brain development. It is when the brain 'wiring' is laid down and thousands of neurons are connecting with 80 per cent of the brain cells a person will ever manufacture occurring in the first two year old life.

Humans are the only species born with such a premature, under-developed brain and it is the first five years where trillions of connections between the brain and cells are being made. It's like an electricity grid that every time something is ignited and sparked – a new connection is made. Every time we interact with our kids or they discover something new a new 'wire' is formed. If building the brain during this crucial time 'goes wrong', the deficits can be permanent.

Look at this photo (Fig. 2) of two three-year-old brains. What is the difference? The one on the right suffered serve neglect and abuse by its mother as a child.

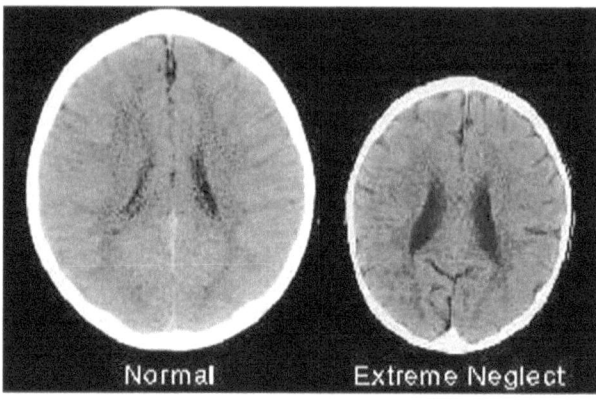

Fig. 2: Three-year-old's normal brain compared to a brain where the child suffered severe neglect

For neurologists, the differences between these brains are remarkable and shocking. The brain on the right is considerably smaller and has areas that haven't formed like the one on the left. The child on the right lacks some of the fundamental building blocks for intelligence. It is more likely they will fail at school, have an addictive personality, and be involved in violent crime. It is more likely they will be unemployed and dependent on welfare, less likely to be able to empathize with others and will more likely develop mental and other serious health problems.

Professor Allan Schore, of UCLA who has studied brain development in babies, stresses that the growth of a baby's brain cells is a 'consequence of an infant's interaction with the main caregiver, usually the mother. He also concludes that the growth of the baby's brain 'literally requires positive interaction between mother and infant. The development of the cerebral circuits depend on it'.

It is during this first five years that our children need to know they are loved, in a safe environment and stimulated enough to promote healthy brain architecture. We are building our relationship with them and at the same time promoting mental resilience.

DEVELOPMENT OF LANGUAGE AND SPEECH

The other major development happening in these early years is the development of language and speech. While children are developing their cognitive skills, they are also developing their ability to learn words and communicate.

It is one of the most exciting milestones when our child says their first word and I love remembering each one of my children's. My youngest daughter could say mum and dad, but her first real word was 'bagel'. We had just moved to America and bagels had become our standard breakfast. My husband was in the kitchen and asked her, at age 11 months, what she wanted for breakfast like he did every morning and she answered 'bagel'. It was a priceless moment.

Children will pick up language and speech around them without too much intervention as their little brains connect. Providing a rich language environment and regular opportunities to interact will give children the best chance to communicate well and develop their vocabulary.

Here are 8 ideas to help your child develop their speech and language.

1. Talk to your child all the time – Even as babies, talk to your child at every chance. The more they hear you talk, and the more vocabulary they hear, the more easily they will pick up sounds and the intonation of the language we are speaking.

2. Encourage a dialogue – As young as 3 or 4 months, you can have a conversation with a baby. They are learning turn taking at this age so hold your baby close and speak then stop. They will speak back in their goo-goo gaa-gaa and they you speak again. You are modeling listening and speaking right from this young age.

3. Read books – Language is rife in books and it is a great way to expand their vocabulary and make the connections between written word and language.

4. Sing songs – Kids will learn a song quickly and love the music and rhythm that go with it. Sing nursery rhythms and even listen to the radio to sing pop songs or music CDs in the car. We had the Wiggles on repeat for many years.

5. Play games – During this fun time of interaction, you are talking and communicating most of the time and they are talking back. It might still sound like gooblygook at a very young age, but they are getting the idea of communicating and interacting with you. Games encourage this dialogue, like Peek-a-Boo, Incy Wincy Spider on their hand or This Little Piggy Went to Market on their toes.

6. Encourage, don't discourage – If your child tries to say the word 'dog' and says 'og', repeat it, rather than correcting it. Say 'yes that is a big dog'.

7. Make every opportunity a language learning time – Through play and simple daily interactions, we can teach our children new language skills. When you are out, point to signs on the road like 'stop' and say 'Look at the stop sign'. Sing nursery rhymes to help them understand rhyming patterns, read rhyming books and allow them to finish the last rhyming word, at the supermarket name each fruit or vegetable you pick up to associate the name with the item.

8. Use flash cards – If you think this will benefit your child and it is a fun game, you might want to use animal flash cards and have them say the name of the animal or the sound of the animal as you flick through the cards from a young age.

All the while, you are developing your child's literacy skills to ensure they are good readers, listeners and learners.

FIND THE BEST CARE FOR YOUR CHILD

It is not surprising that the number of parents working has increased over the past 30-40 years. In Australia now 90 per cent of all fathers work and 65 per cent of mothers work. So who cares for the children from zero to five year?

There are many options for childcare of children aged 0 to 5 years, but it is imperative to find the right care for your child. Especially given this is the time of major brain development and attachment. To give your child the best head start to developing mental resilience, it is important to choose the right option.

The options are hiring a nanny or au pair, a long day care centre, family day care or an occasional babysitter. It is important to find the care that will suit your child and give them the best start in your financial situation and also dependent on location and logistic.

What about developmental delays in early childhood?

There is no doubt that developmental delays and neurobehavioral problems in our children are on the increase. There is no clear cause or cure right now for many of these conditions; however, there is significant evidence to show that early intervention or therapies in most cases, can give a young child the best chance at school and later in life. Some of the more common delays are speech delays, autism and ADHD.

Speech delays

Speech delays are generally the most common reason for intervention in early childhood and often the easiest to fix. Sometimes it is that a child has heard the wrong sound or formed the incorrect mouth technique to say the word and with some professional help, it will generally correct easily. Speech delays affect reading, writing, forming words and verbally communicating.

When my daughter was 3 and had just started preschool, she was having troubling pronouncing the sounds ch, cl, sh, f, r and th. We lived in America when she was beginning to form her words and communicate from the age of 11 months until 2 and a half years and she was listening to everyone around here. We also often had a Filipino babysitter who spoke English well but in a different accent again. A speech therapist worked with my daughter for 6 sessions in collaboration with us doing sound work at home and it was amazing to see the transformation in such a short time.

My son had a stutter when he was also three that lasted for a couple of months. It seemed his little, developing brain was working faster than his words were forming and so he would stutter on r's or l's. By giving him time to speak his words and speaking the word back to him, we didn't need a referral to a speech therapist.

When should you get help from a speech pathologist?

- If you are worried about your child's speech
- If you think your child is slower to form words than peers or siblings
- If you are not understanding them clearly
- If they are three-years-old and not talking well
- If your child's daycare, preschool or school teacher talks to you about it

Children develop their language at different times and it is interesting that 'th' is the very last sound to develop and is often tricky for many kids. There are simple ways to show children how to do this. Demonstrate with your own mouth on where you put your tongue to make that sound and get them to copy it regularly.

Helping your child develop their language provides the best chance to communicate when they are older.

Autism

During the past 40 years children on the autism spectrum have increased ten fold. Now, 1 in 68 American children identify as being on the autism spectrum. That is one child for every two to three classrooms, which is high. Evidence strongly shows that early intervention gives children on the autism spectrum the best chance to develop a higher IQ as well as increasing their social and daily living skills.

There are two major reasons why early intervention is imperative.

As already mentioned, between the ages of zero and five years children's brains are neuron patterning that will stay with them for the rest of their lives. Therefore, if we can work with kids on the autism spectrum before the age of five, there is a more positive influence on the way the brain develops.

The other reason for early intervention is to help children communicate more effectively. More often than not, children on the spectrum are slower to develop their speech than peers, which affects their ability to communicate their needs. If they can't express themselves and get the attention they require to have their needs met, difficult behaviour arises.

What sort of early inventions work best?

The services that are family orientated, well structured and based on sound research and evidence work best for early autism intervention.

FAMILY ORIENTATED. Your child will gain much more from the therapy if the family, or at least a caregiver is involved so it can be integrated and relevant in their day. If your child is in care, involving the daycare centre and preschool is also important and some therapists do sessions at home or in the daycare/preschool setting.

WELL STRUCTURED. The therapist should meet your child where they are at – they should learn new skills and practice old skills. The time you spend together each week should be well organized, predictable and relevant to your child. And there should be regular assessment, monitoring and feedback on the progress of your child. Your child should also feel comfortable in the space and with the provider.

EVIDENCE BASED. The therapy should be specifically designed for children on the autism spectrum. It should be focused on developing attention, compliance, imitation, language and social skills. Depending on the therapy, one component could be to work at reducing difficult behaviour by identifying what lies underneath.

No single therapy will help all children and it will be a matter of finding the best fit for your child and your family.

What Types of Therapies are Available?

Because there is no known cause and no cure for autism, there are so many therapies to help improve the particular symptoms or problems your child faces.

Therapies range from medical, social, behavioural, developmental and family based.

To develop mental resilience and give your child the best chance to learn, speech therapy and development interventions are probably most important for children with autism as they allow your child to communicate which raises their intellectual ability and also their social skills.

Attention Deficit Hyperactivity Disorder (ADHD)

Statistics show three to five children out of every 100 are diagnosed with ADHD in Australia, while in the US it is 11 per cent of all children aged between 4 and 17. That is a total of 6.4 million children in US diagnosed with ADHD! The diagnosis has increased year on year since 1997 with a 53 per cent increase over the past decade. It is more prevalent in boys (13.2 %) than it is in girls (5.6%).

What is ADHD?

ADHD is a behavioural disorder or developmental delay, which results in a child finding it hard to pay attention, be organized, think slowly and sit still. It is categorized into three areas – inattention, impulsive and overactive. Some argue it is not a medical condition, while others argue it is and this is largely because there is no reliable known cause. It is generally diagnosed through comprehensive testing by a doctor, psychologist or psychiatrist.

While the cause of ADHD is not fully known, research points to a number of possible environmental and social factors including:

- Exposure to drugs and alcohol during pregnancy affecting the development of the brain
- Exposure to lead in the first three years of life affecting the development of the brain
- Trauma to the brain from head injury or illness
- Early neglect or issues with attachment to one parent or caregiver between the ages of zero to five years
- Hereditary factors

What do all these factors have in common?
They result in poor development of the parts of the brain that regulate the higher order thinking or executive function including the frontal lobe (including the prefrontal cortex), basal ganglia and the cerebellum – all responsible for thinking rationally.

What are ways to help a child with ADHD? After being fortunate enough to work with children who have been diagnosed with ADHD, these factors are crucial for success with the situation.

- Diagnose early – the earlier a child is diagnosed with ADHD, the more chance there is of having a positive impact on brain development and putting social and academic strategies in place to alleviate many of the symptoms.
- Developing routine, expectations and consistency – Like most children, children with ADHD need to have consistent boundaries in place. They respond more readily to a stable routine and consistency around rules and behaviours.
- Kindness and love – children need to really connect with their parents, teachers or caregivers and feel they have a high sense of significance and belonging within their family and wider community. Being kind and firm at the same time is important.

- Regular exercise – due to the hyperactivity, children with ADHD will often need more time for exercise. This can be a regular trip to the park, structured activities, family bike rides or regular runs around the block.
- Don't expect your child to sit for long periods – children with ADHD generally do not have the attention span to sit through dinner at a restaurant or church on Sunday. Be prepared to take them out or have an alternative arrangement.
- Simple instructions – kids in general can be overwhelmed with multiple instructions, however kids with ADHD with a shorter attention span need simple, one-task instructions. Boys especially respond well to being given simple, bite sized instructions. For example, instead of saying 'before you go to bed, you need to clean you room, brush you teeth and go to the toilet' say something like 'it is time to clean your room'. Once the room is clean, you now need to get ready for bed by firstly cleaning your teeth'. Once the teeth are done, ask if they went to the toilet already?
- Encourage good choices – a lot of the decisions these kids make are on impulse. It is important to help them stop and think before they act so they make the best choice. Teach them a simple statement of Stop, Think, Do and repeat it each time they are faced with a choice.
- Communicate with the school, daycare or preschool regularly – keep a day book if you need to keep up regular communications between you and the school and hold regular meetings to talk about behaviour management techniques at home and at school.
- Recognize and express emotions in a positive way – teach your children ways to recognize their own emotions and skills to deal with them that don't involve harming self, harming property and harming others.
- Keep building that relationship – this is a given really, but know what your child likes, dislikes, what they are reading, who their

friends are, what sports they like watching or who they identify as mentors.
- Patience – children with ADHD often have amplified behaviours with tantrums, power struggles and physical reactions because of their impulsive nature. Every parent caring for a child with ADHD needs bucket loads of patience and a great support network to have a break when they need it.

INTERVENTION FOR ADHD

There are two well-recognized streams of intervention for ADHD including behavioral therapy or medication (or both). As with autism, the earlier this is diagnosed and treated the better it is for children to develop their intelligence, social skills and emotionally intelligence – ideally before the age of five.

Every case is different; however it is well reported that the overuse of drugs to medicate ADHD is at all-time high with over two thirds of all kids diagnosed using prescription drugs such as Ritalin and Adderall. A teacher once told me that half her class was medicated, which has alarm bells ringing that we as a society are putting too much pressure on our children to perform, over medicating to reach the 'norm' of children or raising a generation of overly anxious children. Receiving good grades and conforming our children to have 'good' behaviour is not necessarily putting the child's need at the heart of the diagnosis. I have seen children medicated and it has slowed their brain enough to sit still. They have finally being able to express themselves, sit still long enough to learn to read and write and their self-esteem and confidence jumped enormously. I have also seen children medicated who are no longer recognizable by character. It really is on a case-by-case basis and required expert medical care to support the transition.

Case study: Kyle and his mum

Kyle and his mum came to a workshop I was running. Kyle had been diagnosed with ADHD recently at the age of 6 and his mum was at her wits end. The father was a miner and would spend 3 weeks a month working at the remote mine and fly home for one week a month. Kyle had a younger brother and sister and his diagnosis had tipped the scales. While they knew he had displayed difficult behaviour for a while, his mum was trying to manage with the little energy she had being a virtually single mum to three kids. Kyle was enrolled in four after school activities and his sisters were in two each. He was a sparky boy topping his grades in maths, English and loved science, especially when experiments were involved but he continually got in trouble in class for talking and not being able to sit on the mat for longer than 5 minutes.

On the playground at school, he had a short fuse and if a child provoked him, he would lash out. He spent many lunch times sitting on the concrete in a 'special spot'. At home, if he hit his sisters, he was sent to his room for time out. He was allowed to come out if he didn't yell for 10 minutes. Every time he yelled out, he had to stay in for another 2 minutes. Sometimes he could spend 45 minutes to an hour in his room. He didn't get any one-on-one time with his Dad because he was away for 3 weeks of every month and when he was home, he was so tired, he would sleep for most of it or run around mowing the lawn, doing jobs in the house and helping out the mum. His anger was a huge concern for the mum and she often lost her cool when he got angry. After extra-curricular activities, a session in his room most days and the preparation for bath and dinner, he wouldn't go to bed until 9pm most nights or sometimes even 10. He played his X-Box and also loved Minecraft before school.

> The only solution his mum and doctor came up with was to medicate him with Ritallin. The mum said that when he was taking his medication, he was much better. He was much less angry, didn't hit his sisters anymore and was improving on the playground. However, he had lost his spark. He was no longer chatty and fun to be around. He was no longer topping the class in Maths and when science experiments came around, he was 'too tired' to participate in them. He didn't enjoy his karate anymore and had to sit down quite often.

Let's look at this situation a little more closely.

Kyle was 6. He was an active boy. His dad was never home. His mum had three children under 6 and was trying to run a household; she was tired and got cranky. He was put in time out away from the family often. His emotions were not validated and he was not taught how to identify what 'angry' even looked like. He was over active and at lunch was made to sit down because he was 'naughty'. He was getting in trouble for not sitting on the mat in class so wasn't feeling the love from his teacher. He was bright and needed constant stimulation. He was tired from doing four after school activities and going with his sisters to two each. He was tired from enduring a daily power struggle with his mum. He was tired from going to bed at 9pm, sometimes 10pm every night and he was over-stimulated at school in the mornings because he had played Minecraft before school.

After working with Kyle's mum and looking at the situation more closely, we put these measures in place over time:

- More quality family time together when dad was home – a walk to the local park together and play or a bike ride together
- A common interest for dad and son – they started going to a

regular football game together when dad was home and made paper planes often
- Firm boundaries around technology – no technology in the morning and only 2 hours over the weekend
- No time outs in the bedroom – we set up a dedicated area in the playroom with the rest of his family with his headphones and favourite music as a 'calm down zone'
- Some time out for mum – she was crumbling under the pressure of acting as a single mum and needed some time out to refill her love cup; this involved a coffee with a friend once a week and her mother-in-law having the children once a week for 1 hour while she walked around the lake or did the grocery shopping on her own. She treated herself with a nice candle to light when the kids were in bed and some tea she loved to drink
- Cancelled one after school activity for each child to give them more down time and less time running around
- Met with the teacher to find new ways to get Kyle running around at lunch, rather than sitting down including finding new consequences for his actions
- Set up a robust nighttime routine that had all three kids in bed by 7.30pm
- Encourage both mum and dad to have more cuddles with their kids to start building that loving, compassionate relationship again

When I finished working with the family, it was too early to tell if Kyle could come off his medication; however his behaviour had calmed down substantially and hopefully within time, he will be able to reduce the medication and return to being happily engaged in his learning again and balance it with less behavioural struggles.

CHAPTER 5

Provide the best education for your child

To complement a positive home learning environment, a nurturing educational environment will help build a child's strong mind.

Providing the 'best' education for your child does not necessarily mean sending them to the most expensive private school or sending them away to boarding school. It means finding the best school or preschool to nurture, encourage and challenge your child. It also means finding a school with similar values to your family's values, ideally close enough in proximity to your home for logistics and friendships and with an instant community you can join and belong to as a family.

School is not just about the academics – however, when we are talking about mental resilience, we want to be able to give our children the best possible chance to learn and have the academic skills to do well in life. To do this, we need to choose the best school for them. This will differ for every child and for every family so there is not any right or wrong here, it is about being informed of the different educational choices so you can make the best decision for your child.

Largely, there are three types of education systems in the Western world including:

- Government education system
- Independent (or non-government) education system
- Homeschooling or Unschooling systems

The majority of students attend government schools. In Australia, 65 per cent attend government schools, while 35 per cent attend independent schools. In the US, 10 per cent attend private schools and in the UK it is less at 7 per cent.

The public education system schools vary greatly across geographical locations, as do the independent schools in most states and countries. The independent schools include faith and non-faith based schools such as Montessori and Rudolph Steiner. It is often a well talked about conundrum for parents choosing which school to send their children to and the debate in the parenting circles is rife between public and private. But, ultimately, the best school is the best fit for your child.

The last options, Homeschooling or Unschooling are growing popularity in the United States and to a lesser extent, in Australia with approximately 3 per cent of school aged children in the US being homeschooled. Homeschooling is teaching the traditional education curriculum and teaching it to children at home. Unschooling is an educational method that advocates learner-chosen activities as a primary means for learning and encourages children to learn from their natural surrounds, rather than from a formal curriculum. Both advocate that children learn at different speeds and support different styles of learners, especially those that might not fit the institutionalized system of traditional education.

Here are some factors to consider when choosing the right school for your child.

- Is there a positive learning environment?
- Is there a focus on academics as well as the whole child?
- Does the school have an inclusive culture?
- Ask around the local area – what are the reviews like from parents who already have children at the school?
- Is presentation and appearance important to you? If so, how does the school look and what is the appearance of the children who tumble out at the end of school day?
- Is there a strong community and avenue to make friends at the school?
- Does the school have a similar culture to your home environment?
- What is their discipline policy? Does it fit with yours at home?
- Do the logistics work? Is it easy to get your child to school from your house? If you work, does it provide after school or vocational care?
- Does your child have a particular strength or need support? Can the school cater for this?
- You can often judge a school by how long the teachers have worked there so ask around.
- Is there a vibrant community associated with the school?
- Will there be familiar children at the school?
- Is it coed or single sex and what are your views on that?
- Could their siblings go there if you wanted them to?
- Walk into a classroom. Is it too busy, too quiet, focused on emotion coaching, focused on academics, arts or science? Will this sort of classroom suit your child?
- Is there a sports program and how often does your children participate?

- Does the playground suit your child? Is it gravel, soft play or on grass? Is the playground large or small for the amount of kids at the school?

All these choices and many more will help you to choose the right school for your child and provide them with the best opportunity to learn and build a strong mind or mental resilience.

Technology and kids: What is the impact?

We are parenting the first generation of children that are saturated by technology so we neither have the hindsight or research to be able to determine the impact of technology on our children's brains and development.

A recent study by Jim Taylor Ph. D and author of *The Power of Prime: The Cluttered Mind Uncluttered* argues that the way we shape our children's relationship with technology is the most important part right now. It is determining the benefits and costs of what devices our children are using and the frequency.

Dr Taylor found this relationship with technology could have an adverse or positive effect on attention span, information overload, decision-making and memory/learning. It can also have an effect on whether our children view their technology as yet another tool in their learning and entertainment or become heavily reliant on their devices for learning and entertainment.

As parents, we need to help our children develop a healthy relationship with technology and allow them to see it as yet another tool to learning and entertainment – along with board games, reading, playing games and outdoor play.

How do we get the balance 'right'?

Dr Goodwin is a Children's Technology and Brain Researcher and works with parents and educators to help them raise kids in this new digital age without fearing or banning technology. She draws on psychological research and evidence, as well as her experience as a schoolteacher and mum to determine how technology is impacting our children.

I interviewed Kristy on how technology affects children's brains and what we as parents can do to lessen the impact on my blog and her insight was both revealing and relieving. She covered the most common misconceptions around kids and technology covering the use of technology, video games (including Mindcraft), safe screen limits and addiction. These were her 5 takeaways debunking the common misconceptions around kids and technology.

INTERVIEW: DEBUNKING THE MYTHS OF
TECHNOLOGY AND KIDS – DR KRISTY GOODWIN
There is a lot of miscommunication and techno – guilt around technology and kids and our job is to leverage it in the best ways possible to support, not stifle the ways our little ones learn and develop.

With the iPad being only 5 years old, we don't have a lot of neuroscientific data but what we do know that every experience our children has shapes and rewires their brains so this is bound to – it is just to what extent.

Myth 1. TV is bad for our children
TV can be really beneficial and helpful for kids if it meets these criteria:
- Very repetitive – e.g. Dora. Dora repeats the tasks over and over again
- Linear – following the same format as a classic narrative
- Slow paced – the rapid-fire action cartoons that children often really like are not beneficial because they are over stimulating their brains.

Parents need to know
- What their kids are watching on television,
- How they are watching it and
- When they are watching it.

Setting boundaries are what, when and how we can limit the negative impacts television has on our children's learning and development.

What your kids are watching is important. Is it age appropriate? Is it educational? Is it slow-paced or rapid-fire?

How they are watching it is important. Be aware of the Digital Zombie effect – that is when children 'space out' in front of a television program and are not using any of the ideas to build on their past experience or interpret it with their filters. Sitting with them on the couch or asking what they are watching reactivates this necessary scaffolding for television to be effective. Also be aware and set boundaries around how long are they watching it.

There are two main times in the day when we need to limit our kids to the rapid fire action cartoons on television and video games – before school and 90 minutes before kids go to bed. These shows over-stimulate their brains for a longer period making it harder to go into a classroom, sit down and concentrate and have also an adverse impact on sleep.

Myth 2. There are safe screen time limits

This is a really common myth and it is not helped by the guidelines that are put out there.

The Federal Department of Health and Ageing in Australia and the American Academy of Pediatrics have similar guidelines that recommend the following;

- No screen time for under 2 year olds
- 2-5 year olds 1 hour per day
- 5 and above 1-2 hours per day

There are challenges with these guidelines:

Firstly, they are including ALL screens and assuming all screen time is equal: that is television, iPads, interactive whiteboards at school, X-Box and computers. A child who is interacting with a whiteboard at school is having a whole different experience than if they are passively watching television.

Secondly, these limits have come out as part of an anti-obesity policy saying that if your children are watching screens it is a trade-off for exercising. This is often not the case. When technology is seen as a tool for learning or an experience, it is about parents balancing the tools and experiences with many different activities.

Thirdly, media usage guidelines set up a false economy, lulling parents into a safe zone of thinking it is fine to let our children watch one to two hours of television a day without taking into account when, what and how this is being consumed.

Recent figures shows 80 per cent of Australian families are exceeding the daily limits, so while we need some guidance, the current standards are not working.

However, children under 2 should have screen time limited. 'Don't be in a hurry to dunk your child into the digital stream. Those first 2000 days are vital for brain development and rich language experiences; reading and communicating are essential for building these connections'.

Some sensible guidelines around screen time usage are:

- Ask 'Is this technology enhancing my child's learning or providing age appropriate entertainment?'
- Is my child using lots of different activities and tools for their learning and entertainment and technology is just one of these?

Myth 3. Video games are harmful for kids (including Minecraft)

Lots of parents are bamboozled with their kids use of video games and Minecraft because they don't understand the obsession or how to stop the 'techno-tantrum' that often happens when they are asked to turn it off.

So why is Minecraft just so popular?

Firstly, it is unlike any other video game in its set up. We grew up in a world of Pac Man or Donkey Kong where you had very limited choice of turning left or right or going up and down and when you died often, you would have to go back to the start. With Minecraft, there is no end. There are no levels, just many new worlds of exploring and choice.

Secondly, developmentally children between the ages of 6 to 12 want to explore outside their boundaries and when parents were growing up there was an infinite number of ways to explore parks, backyards, and schools and there was opportunity to roam and play. With the many social factors that now preclude our children doing this – parents work longer, it is deemed unsafe to send your kids to the park on their own – children use Minecraft as an outlet to explore. They are trying to replicate this in a digital world looking for opportunities to experience life, roam, explore and test out scenarios in a safe environment and without parental involvement.

Thirdly, the neuroscientific explanation children like Minecraft and most other video games because when they solve a problem or reach the new level, they are rewarded. Their brains release the neurotransmitter dopamine – the feel good hormone and they want more. It feels good for them to get this praise and is either having a knock on effect in our society with children looking for and being over praised or matching up to what is already happening with an over praising of kids. This instant gratification is meeting the needs of our children's brains.

How do we stop the techno tantrum?

While children are receiving this nice little hit of dopamine, they don't want to get off their game so we are seeing otherwise well adjusted 6 to 9 year olds having a techno-tantrum. They are just like toddler tantrums.

- Set up a Minecraft Management Plan – work out when, how and for how long your child can go on Minecraft each day or each week and communicate it well. Once you have set the clear boundaries and expectation, be consistent with it. So if your child can go on Minecraft on a Friday afternoon for one session, make it only that.
- Children get into their psychological state of flow and are so oblivious of what is around them when they are gaming that when we stop them in the middle of something, it feels wrong to them. Wouldn't it be great if we could engage boys in their learning the same way we can engage them in Minecraft?!

Before your child starts a mission on Minecraft, ask them what they are going to achieve in this session and be clear that will be when they turn it off. Or set the expectation that they will stop when Minecraft transitions from day to night.

If you choose the right game for your child that is educational and engaging (not aggressive, anti-social games) and set up the right boundaries and consistency around video games, they can be beneficial.

Myth 4. Screen time causes ADD and ADHD

There is no scientific research to suggest that screen times cause ADD or ADHD. However, there is a correlation – children that have some attention issues do tend to spend more time with screens, but there is not causation research. Is it that their brains are craving the fast paced, rapid movement of screens or is it that the screens are causing the attention issues?

It is not proven either way and ADD and ADHD is a multi-faceted issue that requires behavioural and at times, medical intervention.

Myth 5. Kids are easily addicted to technology

The media love this statement and the truth is – it is a myth. Only a very small proportion of children are formally and medically addicted to technology, it is between 1 and 3 per cent.

Instead what we are seeing is that children have formed some unhealthy screen time habits and relationships with technology that need to be fixed, especially up until the age of 8. And they are reacting to it.

Here is a summary of Dr Goodwin's top tips for building a healthy relationship with technology:

- Set limits right from the BEGINNING. As soon as you hand your smart phone over to your 2 year old, tell them what apps they can go on and for how long.
- Set clear expectations for usage – when, how long, where and how each device will be consumed.
- Be present to know what your child is consuming and to act on any teachable moments that arise from the technology
- Eyeballs are your best filters, however put age appropriate filters on the internet so children can't access unsavory websites
- Open up dialogue and conversation about technology, its impact and usage
- Keep it out of bedrooms – you can't be present in there to see how, what when or how long they are using their screens
- See it as a tool for learning or a tool for entertainment along with all the other tools and activities children can use or do.

By helping our children build a healthy relationship with technology and showing them it is a tool to learning and experience, we are allowing them to develop strong brains and the ability to understand how technology can help, not hinder, their ability to learn.

CHAPTER 6

Develop a strong values and beliefs system

Values help us make judgments on events, activities and decisions each and every day. They are the building blocks for our belief system and allow us to act ethically and with dignity and respect to situations.

Belief systems are the stories we tell ourselves to define our own sense of reality and it helps us make sense of the world around us. It is ever present in our schema. This can be religious, ideological or philosophical or a combination of all three.

So what has this got to do with resilience in our children?

When adversity or stress strikes, we build up the scenario through our memories, values and beliefs system and how we have experienced the world. To be able to respond favourably to a situation, we enact our values and beliefs systems to make sound decisions.

If we set up solid foundations of values and beliefs, it gives our kids another resource or tool to be able to use when challenged.

A child's values and beliefs are set through their family and, to a lesser extent, their school. They are learnt by modeling of behaviours and embedded by the people around them. Young children especially are very impressionable and will generally try to abide by the values or belief set you have set up: it is when they see it for themselves as teenagers and beyond that they may rebel or revel in the system you have designed for them.

So what is your value and belief set? And do you want to impress that on your children?

I often have conversations with parents who are so busy ferrying their kids from place to place and living their life from day-to-day that they haven't stopped to think about the big picture of values and beliefs but it makes so much sense to help our children design the right set now so we can set them up for future. Here are some ideas for setting up family values and beliefs.

1. Develop values together

At the beginning of 2015, we did a huge driving trip from Canberra, ACT to Rockhampton, QLD. We covered more than 5000 kms and had plenty of time to think and play together as a family.

We were staying in an apartment in Hervey Bay in QLD this one particular night and after a great day bike riding up the promenade, some fishing and lots of swimming in the pool and beach, we were having a robust conversation about what we love to do as a family together. It was the 4th of January and as the conversation evolved, my then 9 year old daughter got out a piece of paper and made us write down 4 things about the year ahead;

- What we love to do as a family together
- Places to go and things to do in 2015
- What we want to learn that is new in 2015
- Our family values

Each person contributed to the discussion and our family values looked like this:

Kindness, politeness, compassion, honesty, love, togetherness (teamwork), hardworking (putting lots of effort in), courageous (being brave), community (family), tolerance.

If that is what our family values stand for, I am content to be part of our family. We have the whole list stuck to the playroom wall for our family to read and we went back over it at the end of the year to see what we did achieve in 2015.

Ever since, at the beginning of each year, we have refined our family values, created a page of highlights and family dreams for the next year. They take pride of place on our study wall and we read them often.

2. Make a family values tree
Children do better at utilizing the values and beliefs system we have in place if they know what each of them means. Similar to what we did as a family at the beginning of the year, you could make up a tree with each leaf or branch having the value that is important to the family together and putting it on show somewhere important. You can then go back to the tree and remind them of the values they have modeled throughout the year.

3. Be the role model
As a parent, we need to be the role model for instilling values.

This is a familiar story for many and I have seen it happen often. A little boy and his dad go to the zoo. Children under 4 years of age, get in for free. The dad and 5-year-old boy go to the counter, the dad says 'Ticket for an adult please' and the little boy says 'What about me?'. The dad tells the little boy he is 4, which causes a major protest because he knows he is actually 5.

Does this equate to honesty and integrity?
What about this one. At the supermarket, a mum is scanning the groceries through the self-serve lane. She gets to the watermelon and can't find the 'watermelon' button on the screen so she gives it to her little girl to hold, finishes the shop and walks out – with an unpaid watermelon. When questioned by the little girl, she says she couldn't find the button and they should have made it clearer so the watermelon is free today.

Honesty, trust?
Another one. A white, Caucasian extended family walk into a restaurant and at the next table is a group of Indian people. The grandmother comments loudly that the Indians at the next table 'smell bad' and are eating badly. She wished they would leave. This is a true story.

Respect, non-judgmental, compassion?
Another one. A family goes to the local shops and there are a lot of homeless people around. They are always begging for money and the dad says 'I am so sick of these homeless people always begging. Why don't they go out and get a real job?'.

Fairness, compassion, non-judgmental?
Another one. Your child has just fallen over and accidentally knocked down your pot plant outside your home. They are crying, with the other children watching on and you yell 'You stupid boy! You are in trouble for knocking down my pot plant, now get to your room'.

Compassion, empathy, shaming, role modeling?
Another one. At the shops, you find an-almost-brand new pair of sunglasses on the floor of the supermarket. Do you hand them in at

the checkout or do you put them in your handbag? Are the kids watching?

Trust, honesty, ethical?
Last one. Your child doesn't want to go to school because they have a big test on so you let them stay at home.

Hard working, risk taking, courage?
Whatever value you deem to be ethically important as a person or as a family, practice it in front of your child.

4. Find a community with shared values and beliefs

If your community has similar values and beliefs to you or your family, it is often easier to engage, continue to teach your family's values and beliefs and, often more fun. This may influence the school you choose for your child or the sporting clubs or even where you live. It is about finding a balance rather than being to set and rigid in values and beliefs that they can't be change or altered.

A belief system is also important. It is another tool or resource for our children to use when they are faced with a difficult situation or decision. This allows them to make good choices when faced with risks such as taking drugs, driving under the influence or breaking the law. It is also a guiding principle to live life by.

What is your belief system? Are you instilling it in your children? Or giving them a choice or exposing them to options to set up their own?

To a certain extent, food choices can be a belief system. A friend of mine has decided the best way to feed her family is to go raw and fresh. That means there are vegetables, fruit, good meat, eggs and nuts. No packaged snacks, limited carbohydrates and sugars. She has made this choice for her children. It is an ideology around food and it will be interesting to see how they react to it when they are able to make their own food choices as teenagers or young adults.

Religion is a belief system. When we lived in America, we were friends with a Mormon family and their beliefs around most things in life were very different to ours. However, it was a chance to challenge our own ideas and beliefs and help our children do the same.

Beliefs and values are different from one family to a next – however it is important to help our children establish a robust system to go by when making choices and bouncing back from adversity.

CHAPTER 7

Build up a bank of positive memories

We view our world through our past experiences and memories. Every person reading this book will take away something different because of your own world constructs or your schema. Our schema is a cognitive framework or concept that helps organize and interpret information – it enables us to react to a situation or information from of our pre-existing beliefs and ideas.

The theory of schemas and its relevance to a child's stage of development was introduced by Theorist Jean Piaget who explained that schemas exist in our brains as a category of knowledge. Building a schema is also the process of acquiring that knowledge. As experiences happen or new information is presented to a child, new schemas are developed and old schemas are changed or modified.

For example, if your child sees a rainbow for the first time and it is full of colour right over the harbour and you get excited about it, they will associate this rainbow with beauty, joy and happiness. The next time they see a rainbow; they will associate it with the beauty, joy and happiness remembering the first one. This will be their schema on rainbows. However, if your child sees a rainbow for the first time and it is raining, cold and only small and you don't get excited by the wonder of a rainbow – it will have been an ordinary experience and they will associate the next rainbow with this experience. They might think it is just another rainbow and miss the beauty and awe.

How do schemas relate to resilience? If we help our children build up their schemas with positive experiences and great memories, when they do encounter a bad experience, they will already have built up a positive back of information and memories to be able to use as a trigger to bounce back to something good.

If we take our children on nature walks and love our time together, they will associate nature with something good. They will be generating a positive schema towards nature and walks. So then, if they encounter a snake on one of these walks and are threatened, they will slot it into their schema as a memory with nature walks – along with all of the other wonderful nature walks. However, if you had never been on a nature walk with your child and the child did not have their nature schema built already, then saw a snake on their first nature walk – it might be a hugely traumatic experience.

The point here is that our job as parents is to expose our children to as many fun, positive experiences as we can to build up their schemas and in turn, their response mechanisms to adversity – their mental resilience. Take them places, have fun together as a family and explore the world together.

But how much do our children actually remember from their childhood? Think about what you remember from being a child. Our memories are generally with the emotion around the memory and the people involved rather than the in-depth details. It is not until about the age of three or four that children form accurate memories and can recall their 'earliest first memory' and not until the age of 10 that children's memories crystallize enough to carry these memories into adulthood. Researchers have found that top memories children have are generally the birth of a new sibling and hospitalization – both highly emotional. However, if a family has 8 children and the eldest child has the experience of the birth of each sibling, I wonder how much they would be able to remember of each one?

Babies relate to their world through their primary carer and it is only when they are toddlers that they are able to make the distinction of 'self'. Between the ages of 2 and about 7 or 8, children are largely egocentric and view the world from their own eyes. And it is not until they are older that they actually realize their memories are part of their construct. So up until this point, it is to do with developing memories on emotion and how they feel or developing their implicit memory, rather than their explicit memory.

This is why it is our job as parents to create positive memories for our children to help them make their own meaning of the world around them.

Here are some ideas to do together as a family to build up positive memories for our children and give them a 'feeling' to bounce back to:

- Go on a family bike ride around a lake or on a bike path
- Pack a picnic and go somewhere lovely to have it – or just set your rug up in the front yard and eat outside together
- Go out for breakfast together
- Go swimming at the beach or walk along the shore
- Take the kids to the museum or aquarium
- Go for a drive in the car to a brand new park or beach
- Take a boat ride together
- Go bowling
- Get out into nature as much as possible and describe the wonder and awe to your children
- Go on a family holidays
- Find your community
- Play board games together

- Create a family ritual at the dinner table each night (For example, add to the gratitude wall, take turns in 'favourite part of the day' or create a WWW board and ask what went well at the end of each day)
- Give lots of cuddles, tickles, rough play, love and use a kind voice
- Buy experiences, not presents

The balance is to not let your own negative scheme get in the way of your child's. Just like our children, we have built up our own schema that shapes our view of the world – be it positive or negative. The trick is to allow our children to build their own schema and not cloud it with our own.

The classic example is if you had a bad experience as a child, you consciously or more likely, subconsciously tend to impose that on your child. When you were little you might have had a negative experience with a bird. When you see a bird, you move away, get scared and react from your own experience. It is easy to impose this negative association you have with a bird onto your children and they will equally be scared of birds. My cousin is terrified of magpies – because her mum is. She is now 18 and can't even sit outside if there is a magpie around. This can also happen with cats and dogs.

Children need to build their fears, dislikes, joys and association to fun from their own experiences to construct meaning.

A friend of mine works at a school as a relief teacher. She was teaching the same class for a week and on the last morning she had a visit from the Principal to explain why she had sworn at a child and slapped her on the arm. As a professional teacher, of course this wasn't the case but the mother was adamant her son had told her this had happened. The teacher spoke to the little boys mother and it became clear that the mother had in fact, had a terrible experience with a casual teacher when she at school and so had been asking negative question about his experience each day. His behaviour in class wasn't perfect so he had been reprimanded, but when pressed by his mother, he gave the worst-case scenario and the mother feed the story. He was enjoying the attention and prompts and continued it.

It was the negative biases coming through from the mother's experiences that had prompted her to ask these questions and assume he was having a terrible week. However, the teacher felt she had formed a good relationship with this boy and was taken aback with the parent's negative views. If the mother had kept her own biases at bay here and asked the her son about the positive aspect of the week, it would have been a different picture.

My mother had long plaits when she was a little girl in primary school. So long that the boys sitting behind her in class would dip her plaits into the inkwells and she hated it. It would take her forever to get the ink out. She had to sleep in plaits and having long hair when she was little wasn't a great experience for her.

So when I was little – subconsciously my mum kept my hair really short. It my preschool photos I had boy short hair and never had it any longer than a bob right through primary school. My own girls have long curly hair and probably wish they had short hair! Perhaps theirs is long because I had short hair. This is a simple example of how our own views and experiences can shape the views of our children – rather than letting them go out and find construct their own meanings and make their own choices we cloud them with our negative schemas.

On a larger scale, imposing our own schema on our children can come in the form of racism, sexism or ridicule against certain religions, groups of people or ideas and opinions. While you will naturally impose some of these ideas in the form of values and as a family on children, largely they need to construct their own meaning and be exposed to differences to form their own schema and views around life.

CHAPTER 8

Encourage a growth mindset and positive outlook on life

'There are only two ways to live your life. One is as though nothing is a miracle. The other is as through everything is a miracle.'
– ALBERT EINSTEIN

Children, and adults alike, are more likely to be resilient if they have a positive outlook on life and optimism for the future. Positive psychology puts optimism and hope as one of its core values for living a happy life. Optimistic people are able to quickly see the positives of life when something bad happens and look to the future. Having a positive outlook puts problems and worries into perspective for our children and protects them from overwhelming, negative thoughts. These are ways to teach our children to be optimistic and have hope.

1. BY BEING A POSITIVE ROLE MODEL

Our children will learn their inner voices from us. If we have a positive outlook and respond to adverse situations in a positive, realistic way, our children will most probably follow our lead. We have already armed them with ways to deal with their emotions and this will allow them to see the Green feelings more often.

2. Use the growth mindset to change negative thoughts into positive thoughts

World-renowned Stamford University psychologist, Carol Dweck first introduced the idea of the growth mindset after years of research to help us reframe the way we solve a problem and the way children learn at school. It is the idea that we can grow our brain's capacity and ability to learn and be motivated to succeed by the language we use, rather than having a fixed mindset about a problem or challenge.

This concept is used throughout many schools and as parents, it could be used in conjunction with your school or as a way to encourage children to try new things and endure setbacks to grow their mind.

Every time our children overcome a challenge, learn something new or are pushed outside their comfort zone, the neurons in their brain are forming newer, stronger connections, and over time they get smarter or grow their mindset.

For example, one of the students I taught in Year 3 thought she was hopeless at Maths. She was a bright girl, however had missed some of the basic concepts when she had changed schools and so had the view that she was bad at Maths. After working on a growth mindset and getting her extra help with the concepts she had missed over a period of two terms (or almost six months), she had a major breakthrough and was put into the top Maths group.

We are also teaching our children here how to fail, recognize their mistake, learn from it and move on. One way to do this is to reward and praise children's effort, their strategies used to solve a problem, their focus, their perseverance and improvement – rather than praising or rewarding their intelligence or talent. Just like disciplining then, we are praising the activity and strategies, rather than the person.

This is what a growth mindset chart (Fig. 3) might look like in a school and could be adapted for home.

DEVELOPING A GROWTH MINDSET

INSTEAD OF.....	TRY THINKING....
I'm not good at this	What am I missing?
I give up	I'll use a different strategy
It's good enough	Is this really my best work?
I can't make this any better	I can always improve
I made a mistake	Mistakes help me to learn
I just can't do this	I am going to train my brain
I'll never be that smart	I will learn how to do this
Plan A didn't work	There's always Plan B
My friend can do it	I will learn from them

Source: Carol Dweck (2015), The Secret to Raising Smart Kids, Scientific American Mind

Fig. 3: An example of developing a growth mindset chart

3. Catch these negative thoughts early

Once we get in the habit or pattern of negative thoughts, it is much harder to shift them. So help your children catch their negative thoughts early. Every time they think something is too hard or too bad, help them reframe their thinking. There is no need to be Polly Anna here, however realistic, positive thoughts go along way further than negative thoughts. These thoughts are also shaping our child's inner critic. The negative thoughts can escalate into an unrealistic catastrophe. To help our children be kind and positive in their thoughts now helps shape them as adults too.

For example, mindset around body image is very important from a young age. Children as young as five years have said they are 'fat' and it has had dire consequences on eating habits, eventually leading to anorexia. Promoting a positive body image is important and catching any negative thoughts early on to help with as a parent or to get professional support.

4. SAY YES MORE OFTEN

Having a laugh and some fun with your children lightens up the mood and helps them experience a positive outlook. When they are having fun, they are not thinking about worries and problems – they are immersed in the fun moments.

Life gets busy and if we are on a frantic schedule, there is little time to be spontaneous and do something fun. However, because our kids live so much in the moment, this is the moment they will remember the most and give them the positive memories to bounce back to when things get tough.

So when your child asks to have a play at the park after school – say yes. When they ask to have an ice cream after the play at the park – say yes. If you go to the beach and you haven't bought their swimmers and they ask to go in – say yes. You can dry them. Our children will remember these fun moments. They won't remember the car trip to the next tennis lesson or the time you had to go home to fold the washing and cook dinner. These things are important too; however building positive childhood memories help our children have the schema to bounce back.

Slow your weeks down enough to be able to have these spontaneous fun times together as a family. All the while you are building your relationship with your children in these fun times – so it is a win-win.

5. TEACH OUR CHILDREN TO FAIL BY TAKING A RISK OR LEARNING SOMETHING NEW

Each year we go on a beach holiday and this year, my husband taught our children to surf for the first time. They have used boogie boards, but never a board they could stand up on. He hired a board from the local surf shop and we all went down to the beach. There was lots of chatter between them with nervous anticipation. My youngest went first and she got onto her knees by her third go. The other two had a first got to their knees and then eventually stood up. My youngest daughter was determined to stand up when it was her turn next and she did. They surfed wave after wave – sometimes they stood and sometimes they got dumped. After a whole morning in the surf, they were bubbling with excitement about learning to surf and their self-confidence and sense of achievement was at an all time high. They had mastered a new skill and were already talking about the next time on the board.

By learning and mastering this skill, the kids failed and achieved and failed and achieved and tried again and again to stand up. They kept on going. They were learning it is OK to fail – this is a crucial life long lesson our children need to learn to be able to bounce back from adversity. At some point in life, we all fail. It is these failures that most often lead us to our greatest successes. If we teach our kids to fail well, we are helping them to be mentally resilient.

6. Teach Gratitude

The definition of gratitude is the quality of being thankful and a readiness to show appreciation for and return kindness. Having good manners and saying thank you is not enough, it runs deeper. It is a real intention of acknowledging that what you have received is treasured and appreciated.

The opposite of gratitude is entitlement and it is constantly said we live in the age of entitlement where our teenagers and young adults expect everything to be handed to them on a silver platter. Will this sense of entitlement help our children bounce back? Probably not.

According to gratitude expert, Robert Emmons when things are going well, gratitude allows us to celebrate and magnify the goodness. However, when things are going badly, this is when gratitude really kicks in.

"In the face of demoralization, gratitude has the power to energize. In the face of brokenness, gratitude has the power to heal. In the face of despair, gratitude has the power to bring hope. In other words, gratitude can help us cope with hard times," said Robert Emmons.

Emmons's research shows that when children, between the ages of 10 to 19, practice gratitude they feel a greater life satisfaction, more positive emotion, have higher levels of optimism and feel better about life and school. More importantly, it helps our children build resilience – the skill most needed to bounce back from adverse situations or stress.

These are some practical ways to instill a sense of gratitude in your children

- Find the favorite part of the day. When you are all together as a family, usually at the dinner table at night, go around the table and ask, "What is your favorite part of the day?" This allows your children to look for the positives in their day, rather than the negatives. As they get older, you can change this to, "What are you grateful for?"
- Keep a gratitude jar. At some stage each day, have your children write down or draw what they are grateful for. Put it in the jar each day and at the end of the month or end of the year or in a particularly rocky time, pull them out to read as a family.
- Don't buy everything your children ask for. – Even if you can afford it, don't always buy your children what they ask for. Get them to save their own money or wait until a birthday. This teaches delayed gratification and allows your child to be more grateful for what they receive.
- Embrace the "gratitude teachable moments." These are the moments when you can remind your child how they can be grateful (not why they should!). It might be when you see a rainbow together or have a spontaneous play date – remind them to be grateful for the moment they have shared and the beauty they saw or enjoyment they had.

- Be a role model for gratitude. Show your own gratitude for what you receive and talk to your children about it. Show that it is often more important to give, rather than receive.
- Make "thank you" a sincere word, not just a learned word. From the age of 10 months, we can teach our children to say 'ta' and get into the habit of manners. However, from the age of 3 or 4 onwards, talk to your children about what 'thank you' actually means and why they are saying it.
- Show your kids how other people live. Give them opportunities to be in different communities and help them understand how other people live.
- Don't go overboard on giving presents. In a world full of "stuff," it is easy to get to a birthday or Christmas and overload our children with presents. Our children don't need lots of presents to have a special time on these days and they will often only play with a few things and leave the other toys anyway.
- Open the card *before* the present. It is a strict rule in our family that when you receive a present, you always open the card first. Then it becomes more about who is giving the present, rather than what you are receiving.
- Send a thank you card to a teacher or coach. When the season ends or the school year is over or just because, have your children write a thank you note to their teacher or a coach with reasons why they are grateful for what that person has done for them.
- Show love with "presence, not presents." The commodity of "time" is the most precious thing you can give your children. They don't need lots of stuff and presents. If you go away, don't come back with presents, come back with an hour of cuddles or an hour of talking.

Graham Long, a pastor from the Wayside Chapel, tells a great story of how he would always bring a sweetie or small gift home from work each night for his small son. This one night he had had a busy day and forgot the gift. His son riffled through his pockets and found nothing. His son had a huge tantrum and all he had to offer was love.

- Keep a gratitude journal together (or a count your blessings journal). From the age of about 10, you and your child or children could keep a Gratitude Journal together. Each night, write down 3 things you are grateful for from the day and talk about it.
- Encourage your kids to help out without being asked. If you encourage your kids to see something around the house and help out with it, without being asked, this will become a habit to cultivate in society when they are older.
- Teach the difference between "necessity" and a "luxury." This is the same as teaching our children the difference between a "need" and a "want." When you are next in the supermarket with your children and they start asking for different items to put in the trolley – classify the item as a 'need' or a 'want' and discuss how the want will enhance their day.

7. APPRECIATE NATURE

Revel in the wonder of a rainbow. Listen to the birds. Look at the flowers in spring. Hear the rain on the roof. Wonder about what makes the waves crash. Walk bare foot in the sand often. Taste the snowflakes as they fall. Grow a plant in the soil. Nurture the plant and help it to thrive. Jump in muddy puddles. Stand in creeks. Catch tadpoles. Find ladybugs. Hold worms from the garden and put them back in their home. Look at the blossoms and notice how they change each day. Lie in piles of leaves in autumn. Swim in lakes, rivers and oceans. Climb trees and rocks. Look over the city or countryside from the top of a mountain or look out. Go for a walk through the forest. Explore nature. Watch the stars twinkle. Know the moons cycle. Chase the Aurora Australis. Feel the wind blowing through your hair.

Knowing and appreciating nature can help our children turn from the 'down of life' to the 'up of life' by being captured by the awesomeness and the sheer size and scale of the world we live in.

8. INSPIRE HOPE AND OPTIMISM IN YOUR CHILDREN

> *'Optimism is a strategy for making a better future. Because unless you believe that the future can be better, you are unlikely to step up and take responsibility for making it so'* ~NOAM CHOMSKY

Hope and optimism put our children's challenges and setbacks into perspective. With the hope and optimism of a new day dawning each and every day, we can overcome the biggest of challenges by seeing that life will go on and the next day will be brighter than this day or the next moment or the next month. To dream and have optimism is to realize that there is a higher power at play here and we need to stay strong to keep the dreams and hopes alive. It is an overall, big picture strategy to build and develop resilience and goes hand in hand with positive thinking and a bright outlook on life.

> *'Just when the caterpillar thought the world was over it became a butterfly.'*

CHAPTER 9

Build self-esteem and self-confidence

People with a high self-esteem and self-confidence are better able to bounce back from setbacks and adversity because they believe in themselves and back their decisions. They are also less likely to experience the major lows because they have a positive inner critic and are able to find joy in their strengths. They are also more likely to try new things, experience risk and failure and seek and harness positive opportunities. Helping our children identify their strengths and encouraging them to balance them with their life as well as helping them find their joy will promote healthy self-esteem and self-confidence.

1. IDENTIFY AND ENCOURAGE STRENGTHS

> *'We change the world by tiny individual acts of honesty, courage, kindness, integrity, by celebrating our strengths, just a little more each day, and helping others do the same.'* JENNY FOX EADES

Our kids will naturally be better at some things than other things. By finding and developing their natural talents, skills or knowledge, we are allowing our children to find their source of motivation and also their joy and self-confidence. According to psychologist and author, Dr Lea Waters in her new book 'The Strength Switch', she defines strengths as doing something that is energizing, performed well and performed often. Strengths can be categorized by intelligence, talents, skills, character or relational abilities.

Doing well in their own strength will allow our children to experience moments of self achievement, self confidence, self worth and know what really motivates them to push harder and do better. They will also solve problems so they can naturally do better on their own and this encourages goal setting and intrinsic motivation to succeed which will carry them in their study, work life and even relationships. They are developing their own rules around the expectations they set for themselves without us encouraging or discouraging. They are realizing peer relationships and pressures to succeed in their area of strength.

This also threads back to building positive memories for our children so they can bounce back to this place in their mind when needed. If we identify their strengths and they have successes, they are creating their own schema around soccer or gymnastics or drums – whatever it is they can do well.

So how do you find this strength?
Try many new things and often. Expose children to different opportunities to play team sports, individual sports, learn an instrument, and play in the chess club but not all at once!

Strengths in our children will change as they grow and develop. Some may only last for a few months and some many years, depending on their interest and our encouragement. Our children will tell us how long to encourage these strengths and when to look for new ones. A strength may develop out of sheer determination to do really well at something or there might be a break through moment when they weren't so good at Mathematics before, but now they understand the concepts and have been propelled to the top group at school. Mostly these strengths will develop out of a natural ability to do well in a certain sport, subject, talent or in the Arts.

If a child finds a strength, don't limit it to just that activity. Keep them exploring new areas of achievement so they don't get fixated on this one area of achievement at the expense of all others as it would then be counter-productive.

It doesn't just have to be a talent, skill or level of knowledge, but a strength in a child's character that they can have a lot of wins around will also work. If your child is truly empathetic and develops friendships easily – this is her character strength to harness. Your child might be naturally curious, encourage it. Hope, kindness, emotional intelligence, self-control and perspective all help to bounce back from stress and trauma. Other character strengths to develop or build on include appreciation, bravery, gratitude, forgiveness, fairness, leadership, teamwork, love and honesty.

2. Leave time for kids to be bored – don't over schedule your kids!

Journalist and leading international advocate for the Slow Movement, Carl Honore knows all about the dangers of over scheduling our children. Recently, Carl coached three families in Australia for his television documentary, *Frantic Family Rescue* to slow down the pace of their lives and find 'joy and serendipity together'.

While it is important to find and nurture our child's strengths to help with confidence, enjoyment and self-esteem – it is not doing our children any favours to put them in activity after activity. However, it seems that middle class Australian families are investing a huge amount of money and time to develop these high achieving kids, and its not just in Australia – it's across the Western world.

Families on average travel 12,600 kilometres per year to extra curricular activities, half way to the moon by the age of 16 years!

Carl coached a family with an 8-year-old son who was doing 16 extra curricular activities a week including ballroom dancing, nippers, little athletics, piano and maths tutoring. He was clearly tired and his mother was getting cross with him for not doing everything to perfection.

In my own classroom, I taught an 8-year-old boy who started to fall behind in his reading and maths and was having major issues on the playground. As it turned out, with two full time working parents he was doing three codes of football a week, karate, tutoring, learning drums and spending until 6pm most nights in after school care. His whole world was crashing down on him because he was exhausted. So when he was on the playground and someone took the ball off him in soccer, he had nothing left in his petrol tank to deal with it. His emotions were running high and his little mind was over tired. In addition, he would spend any spare time playing Minecraft on his computer. He would come into my classroom exhausted and I would expect him to finish his maths and writing because he was a bright boy – but he just couldn't. He couldn't bounce back from any stress or adversity coming his way because he was over scheduled and over tired.

> *Children's brains are hard wired to play. They need to get away from adults and be the protagonists of play.* ~ CARL HONORE

Now, 60 per cent of our children's play is structured. Children need time to explore, imagine, create and interact with others in an unstructured way. This is how they develop their risk taking skills, navigate tricky relationships, make mistakes and have some autonomy and independence to make choices away from adults. These skills are all invaluable to developing resilience.

One of the other families in Carl's F*rantic Family Rescue* documentary had three children and between them had activities from

7am to 7pm each day during the week and a similar schedule on the weekend. This left no time to enjoy a relaxed family meal together, trips to the park or beach, having fun together or really connecting on any level, except in the car.

Carl gave each family a 'slow fix' remedy and for a month, they weren't allowed any screen time, had to have a family meal together once every day, reduce extra curricular activities to one per week and the car isn't to be used for trips less than 2 kilometres from their house – they had to walk or ride.

After Carl worked with the families for the month, most of the results were positive. However, the family with the 8 year old boy sadly couldn't follow the schedule Carl set and went back to their old ways of having 16 extra curricular activities a week because the mother wanted to keep pushing her children to over achieve. Her reasoning was that she didn't have the opportunity as a child to do any of these activities and her children's wins were her wins, however there was a significant decrease in screen time in the household including by the mother.

The other two families followed the schedule and thrived. They enjoyed their new found time together. One of the boys in the families said he was loving riding his bike to school, walking to his friends place and being out in the fresh air kicking his footy, rather than glued to his X-Box. An important lesson for any child.

While we can't turn back the clocks and raise our children the way we were raised with freedom, autonomy, independence and pretty well free range parenting – we can certainly make changes to spend more time together as a family, connect with our kids on a deeper level and allow our kids to be kids. This gives their brains time to build mental resilience and the extra skills needed to bounce back.

So how do you balance the scheduled vs. non-scheduled time for your kids?
New York Times journalist Bruce Feiler explored this notion of finding the balance in his article *Overscheduled Children: How Big a Problem?* Following interviews with psychologists and childhood experts, he drew the conclusion that the motives behind children doing extra curricular activities and the parent's reactions were the main issue. The parents were pushing their children to do an activity because they did it as children or they think it is 'good for the child'.

According to clinical psychologist and the author of *The Pressured Child,* Michael Thompson the balance is 'finding the line between a highly enriched, interesting, growth-promoting childhood and an overscheduled childhood'. Michael notes the real problem is that highly successful, time poor parents with a high degree of control over their own lives, take control of there children's lives putting them in extra-curricular activities they WANT their child to do– without taking the interest of the child into account.

Another view point from psychology professor at Columbia University, Suniya Luthor, who has done extensive research into the role of extra-curricular activities in children's lives, concludes that scheduling children is good for having well rounded activities outside of academics and opportunities to hone their skills. However, problems arise when parents over scrutinize the performance of their children in the activity and make it overly competitive.

Dr Polly Young-Eisendrath, a clinical psychologist and author of *The Self Esteem Trap* argues that too many activities are problematic for children as it detracts from a child's natural development affecting their self-confidence.

> *'Children really need that time to lie around, play more freely and have periods when they are side-by-side with their parents'.*
> DR POLLY YOUNG-EISENDRATH

With these alternative views, it is important to balance your child's schedule so they have enough time to allow to play freely, sleep well, eat well, have time to breath, fit homework in, do fun things together as a family AND do fun extra curricular activities that excite them and give THEM joy.

A good indicator of whether your child should be doing a particular activity or not is how much they are enjoying it. If they are going off dragging their feet to their activities, don't send them – it has to be fun or it is counter-productive. If parents are pushing their kids into an activity because they did it as kids, or pushing them to do it to live through the wins of the children or even to keep up with the other families at school who are doing every activity imaginable – then don't it.

Guidelines for extra-curricular activities

- If your child is 0-5 years, one scheduled activity per week is plenty and it may only be for a winter or summer sport or not at all.
- When your child starts Kindergarten, do not schedule any activities for the first term and then one or two in the following terms. They need time to settle into the routine of school and are often very tired in this time.
- If your child is 5-12 years, two scheduled activities per week are plenty.
- If you have multiple children, balance it out over the year between summer and winter sports so you ideally are only doing two per child per season.

Each family is different. Each child will have a different ability. There will be different opportunities in your location and different capacities in each family. Choosing your own schedule is important to the wellbeing and thriving nature of your family.

INTERVIEW:
CARL HONORE SAYS SLOW DOWN TO PARENTS

Following the Frantic Family Rescue documentary, I had the pleasure of interviewing Carl Honore for a podcast on my blog. His message is that the frantic pace of our lifestyle is affecting our children – especially their resilience.

'Our children's resilience is being sacrificed on the alter of this smothering, hyper, helicopter approach to parenting – definitely. The one thing you want children to come out with at the end of their childhood is to be able to stand on their own two feet and be resilient. And that is not what is happening anymore.

We are molly coddling, wrapping our children in plastic sheet or cotton wool, raising them almost in captivity – we are not allowing them to run any risks at all. They are not learning how to make mistakes and how to deal with the emotional and physical fallout from screwing up and getting up. Finding the strength to stand up again after a mistake or a mishap and dust yourself down and get on with it without turning to mummy and daddy for help or a grown up to do it for you. And I think this is one of the great disservices we are doing to the next generation.

Virginia Wolf described childhood as that great cathedral space. I think of that as the way most children have always grown up until the last generation. Having that credible freedom to go out and run risks, deal with mistakes and get stronger gradually at their own pace. Rather than being kept in a gilded cage and then suddenly unleashed on the world at the age of 18 to go to university, where of course they can't cope. And this is something you see around the world now.

In universities and colleges are reporting in record numbers, first year and second year kids are just falling apart emotionally. They just cannot cope. They are not aware of all that is going on. Suddenly, having been raised in this bubble of over protection, they find themselves out in the real world and they do not have the resilience and emotional internal reservoir to cope and so they end up falling apart or back on to medication or turning to the grown up world to bail them out. If we allow ourselves to take our foot off the accelerator pedal and just back off and let them get on with it, then our children will emerge far more resilient.

Even simple things like letting them climb trees. Everyone is so afraid of letting their kids climb trees nowadays – in fact in Britain I saw a statistic that showed children in Britain are 3 times more likely to get hurt falling out of bed than falling out of a tree because no one allows their kids to climb trees anymore – it is too dangerous.

Another statistic came out roughly the same time to show that as children successful entrepreneurs – people who are really lighting up the startup world – 80 to 85 per cent of them were veteran tree climbers growing up. It is obvious why. They took those risks, they were able to look up into the complex matrix of all those branches and figure out the path up and if they fell, they got hurt and they got up again. We are constantly saying as teachers, parents and politicians, we want children to be able to do these things but then when it comes to how we raise them, we don't allow them to learn those skills.

There is kind of a weird disconnect going on that I think we can feel intuitively is happening and, because of that as an entrepreneur or optimist we need to turn it around. In fact we are looking at and increasingly finding ways to back off and let children have that childhood that allows them to grow up strong, resilient and tremendously good citizens.

So why has our parenting style changed so much in just one generation? We, in general, had a much freer childhood, almost free range – why has so much changed?

We have stumbled into a unique moment in the history of parenting and childhood for a number of reasons. A number of historical and social trends have intercepted together to be a perfect storm.

The coming down of the Berlin Wall and the globalization of the world economy has created a more competitive environment so parents feel they have got to push very hard to prepare their kids to get ahead, to survive even in this cutthroat world.

Also the changes demographically. We are having children older now than ever before and that makes a big difference. Especially since we are having smaller families. We know from all the research done, especially in China that the fewer children you have, the more anxious you are about each child and then if you have children older, we come to the parenting game with a different ethos. We have spent many years in the workplace. We come into the home environment to start having children and we bring a lot of that workplace culture with us. And we think, we how do we parent better like I would at work. I will invest a lot of energy, put a lot of money in, and ask a lot of experts. Our professional lives become parenting.

There is a lot of guilt as well and of course this naturally tends to be more mothers, find themselves maybe giving up a big highflying, high-pressure career who suddenly find themselves at home and think what do I do now? And they look at their child and think, well there's my new project and so a lot of that energy gets poured into the child and they find it harder to just let things happen, because that is not what you do at work. You don't just let things happen. You get in. You're proactive and that spirit comes back to us in the home now.

Also, technology. Technology has made us expect things to happen at the speed of software and increased our general impatience and that is part of it, too.

The consumerist culture is a contributing factor. It has really ratcheted up over the last generation, so that now we live in a world of soaring expectations where we are perfectionists. We expect everything to be perfect – perfect body, perfect family, perfect house, perfect vacation, perfect kitchen, perfect career – everything has to be perfect, because we are constantly putting up this illusion, an air brushed version of ourselves on Facebook and social media and that creates a lot of pressure on parents as well to create the perfect child. Really the pressure is to create the perfect alpha kid.

And so you put all of those things together and it doesn't surprise me that we have ended up in this extraordinary place where parenting has become a version of product management and product development.

3. FIND YOUR CHILD'S JOY

A 'joy' is something your child will love and cannot put down – it is not necessarily an achievement but something that bring them joy. It is something they love doing and it is our job to find this absolute joy. The positive emotions will carry them through their day. A joy may be the same as a strength or it may be something completely different.

How do you find their joy? You ask them. You ask them what they love doing. You ask them what they would like to do every day and you talk to them about the funniest thing they do in their daily lives.

I asked my 10 year old daughter what she loved doing. She loves exploring and going on new adventures. Awesome. This whole travelling thing is rubbing off. She also loves sport; when I pressed on it, she loves sport she can really enjoy and is not pushed on. She doesn't like swimming because she is pushed too much to do laps and strokes and she wants freedom in her sport. She doesn't want to be in the A team for netball because she wants to enjoy her game. She loves running and won the cross country, so went to 'zone'. Zone is when you race against kids from other schools. She hated it. She never wanted to do 'Zone' again because she was being 'pushed to the limits' (her words). She didn't want to feel the pressure of running to win. She just knew she wanted to run so Little As was perfect. She is good at dance, but doesn't want to do it because it is too prescriptive. She likes dancing at home to the radio. There is something here that tells me she still needs to be pushed to know how to strive, but for now I need to find other avenues to help her strive on her own – not by being pushed. Time to book another holiday.

When I asked my 8-year-old son, he loves reading. He has always been an avid reader and he loves the journey and adventure of the stories. He loves the characters and what they do in the stories and he wanted to be able to read more fiction books. He also loves sport. He loves football, but interestingly, after our conversation, I learnt not football on a Saturday morning organized sport; he loves the football his mates all play at lunchtime on the oval. He loves *that* football. He doesn't like the seriousness and code of 'real football', but the fun, run around lunchtime football with friends. So, at his sleep over for his birthday party, we will make sure there are enough friends, the time and space to play a lunchtime-style game of football together.

If I hadn't had this deep conversation with my kids about what truly lights them up right now, I would have enrolled them in unnecessary sports and put them into something because I thought it was a good idea for them to do it. I have probably already done it. Their joy will change over time and it is important to have this conversation often. It is our job as parents to really ask our kids what they love and then let them do it. Let them find that joy they want to do every day.

Slow Dance
(by child psychologist David L. Weatherford)

Have you ever watched your kids on a merry-go-round,
or listened to the rain slapping the ground?

Ever followed a butterfly's erratic flight,
or gazed at the sun fading into the night?

You better slow down, don't dance so fast,
time is short, the music won't last.

Do you run through each day on the fly,
when you ask 'How are you?', do you hear the reply?

When the day is done, do you lie in your bed,
with the next hundred chores running through your head?

You better slow down, don't dance so fast,
time is short, the music won't last.

When you run so fast to get somewhere,
you miss half the fun of getting there.

When you worry and hurry through your day,
it's like an unopened gift thrown away.

Life isn't a race, so take it slower,
hear the music before your song is over.

CHAPTER 10

Facilitate an understanding of financial matters

By the age of 7, children have already formed their money habits. So why don't we talk to them about it? Money is an integral part of life and yet in many households, talking about money is taboo. Sure, we don't want our kids to necessarily know what our pay cheque is or how financially sound we are in relation to our friends or neighbours, but we do want them to know enough to develop their own healthy relationship with money early and also to know how to equip themselves with financial freedom and stability later in life decreasing their risk of adversity. Here are some ideas to facilitate a healthy relationship with money.

START EARLY. By the age of 3, our children can understand the concepts of spend and save. They have been watching us pay for groceries and exchange money for goods for 3 years now and already know that we use money to buy goods. They know that we need to save money to buy larger items just through listening to adult conversation. The more we talk to our children directly about spending and saving, the more vocabulary they will have around money.

I was teaching a class of 5 year olds about money and how to recognize it. A little girl put her hand up and said 'we don't need lots of money to be happy and people with lots of money spoil their kids'. She had obviously heard these words somewhere, whether it be from her parents or another adult, so it is important we talk to our children about the fundamentals of money early.

LET YOUR CHILD HANDLE MONEY. When you are at the shops, give your child $5 at the check out and let them buy a piece of fruit or packet of biscuits with the money and get the change. Get them to count the change and talk about the coins they used. Or at the coffee shop, let them pay for your coffee (or their babychino). You might set up a fake shop at home or at the park and use real money to buy items. At the park we went to when my kids were really little, there was a counter underneath the slide and we bought pizza, coffees and sandwiches here – the currency was sometimes even bark chips. The more our kids handle money, the more used to it they become. The best way for them to learn about the coins and notes is to see them, touch them and spend them.

EXPLAIN THE PROCESS OF MONEY. Where does money come from? How do we get it in our bank accounts? How do we use that money to buy groceries? What if I don't have the money in there? Talk about money being a finite resource and talk about the different ways you can get money. Traditionally, it is by studying hard at school to get into a good job where you then work hard to make more money. There are different paths and it is important to talk to your kids about this.

TALK ABOUT YOUR BUYING DECISIONS. Give your children an understanding of making decisions and choices over money. If you are at the supermarket, talk to kids about some of the items you are putting in the trolley as being necessity or a luxury. Talk to them about 'specials' or 'discounts' and how they impact on the grocery bill. Talk to them about the different brands and if you buy based on the brand or the cost.

TEACH DELAYED GRATIFICATION. This is getting increasingly difficult to teach as a concept with instant gratification being part of our consumer-driven society. However, it is important to teach our children to wait and build up their money for a big purchase. This doesn't have to be directly related to money and can be taught when waiting for their turn for a swing in the park or not getting the latest game or movie now, but waiting until their birthday or Christmas to get it. This will allow them to build up skills to save their money.

THE IMPORTANCE OF GIVING. You can be the role model for giving and it is important to differentiate here whether you are a person that gives their time or their money. If you donate your money to a good cause, involve your child in the process. My family has sponsored a little girl to get her through her schooling at St Jude's in Tanzania for the past ten years and my parents even went to the school in Africa in 2010 to visit her and meet her family. Each quarter, they send us her school reports with a hand written letter from her to our family. They love reading her letters and can see this donation is improving the life of this little girl. It might be that you give your time for free, instead of giving money – talk to your children about the difference.

SHOULD YOU GIVE POCKET MONEY? It is great for our children to have some money to learn about it, but the big question is: What do they get pocket money for? Many parents believe that children should pitch in and help out around the house as part of a family. Others think it is worthy of being paid to make a bed or walk the dog and it really comes down to your own values and worth over money. Whichever way you choose, it is great for kids to have some money to learn how to spend, save and make early financial decisions.

SET UP A BANK ACCOUNT EARLY. Get your child a bank account early and whether you add money in yourself or get them to add money in, you are creating a great habit of having money in the bank and they feel so grown up!

Author of *The Barefoot Investor*, Scott Pape facilitated the idea of 3 jars. When your children get money as their pocket money or for a birthday, have 3 jars. Label the three jars with 'Spend', 'Save' and 'Give' and encourage your child to divide their money into each jar. Then have a goal with what they will do with their 'spend' jar. They might put the 'Save' straight into their bank account. They might 'Give' their money with a cause or a struggling sibling and the 'Spend' jar might need to grow enough so they can buy a toy or game. We have done this now for the past couple of years. Our children have three jobs to do each week and get a dollar for their age. So, my daughter who is nine years old, has three jobs and to get the maximum amount, must complete all three jobs each week. If she does she gets the whole $9 and divides it into her jars each Sunday night. Is she doesn't do her jobs, she gets a portion of the $9 and divides it between her jars. It has meant they have money to buy what they want to buy with my son saving up for a basketball ring and at one stage they pooled together their 'give' money and donated the $67 to a Go Fund Me page for a family my son played basketball with and who's father died in a car accident. It has been a transformative money experience for all of them and for us to see their individual attitudes to money and healthy sibling competition!

PART 2

Moulding a Brave Heart
(Emotional Resilience)

WHAT IS EMOTIONAL RESILIENCE?

Moulding a brave heart is one of the core traits of building a resilient child.

With a brave heart, our child will have the necessary emotional skills to bounce back from adversity or a negative outcome. Building a brave heart in our children requires teaching our children the emotional skills, setting the best foundation to form strong relationships and developing emotional stability.

Mental, physical and emotional resilience work as both long term and short-term solutions for building a resilient child. Although, when adversity hits, generally our first reaction is an emotional one, so helping our children develop their emotional capacity to react well to an adverse situations is imperative. It rides on many factors and one of them is understanding the natural ups and downs of the pattern of life.

Life has its ups and downs. That is it's natural pattern. While the events, activities or situations that cause the ups and downs or highs and lows can be out of our control, the height of the up and the low of the down are usually governed by how we react to the event, activity or situation or how well we are prepared for it to happen.

Metaphorically, we can't always stay in the 'up', that would be the impulse of an addict. And if we always stayed in the 'down', we would be depressed. The key is finding the balance to move along the continuum so our ups and downs are stable and more importantly, we know how to move from the 'down' to the 'up' again (Fig. 4).

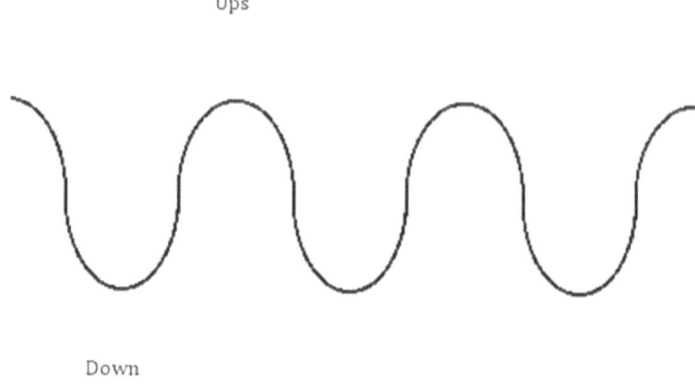

Fig. 4: The patterns of the ups and downs of life

With the right emotional skills in place, our children will know how to deal with the setbacks they face to reach the best outcome – like how to interact with the school bully, get over not being picked in the cricket team, being told they are not good enough for the choir, being called names on the playground, scraped knees, anger, fear, disappointment, resentment, jealousy, deal with the over-excitement of school camp and all the other things our children face in real life.

You could actually replace the words 'ups' and 'downs' in life with 'positive' or 'negative' outcomes and come to the same conclusion. Look at just one day. It is sheer luck if that whole day is met with all ups or all positive outcomes. Look at a year. When we start a year we are optimistic it will be the best one yet, but it has to come with downs as well as ups because that is the pattern of life. To give our children the skills and abilities to know how to manage those downs providing the best opportunity to be strong, healthy and productive adults.

Once our children have formed these skills and practiced and embedded them, they will ideally utilize them when dealing with stresses as teenagers and then into setbacks and adversities in adulthood.

As you can imagine, hitting the 'downs' constantly and not having the skills to get back 'up' is when our children experience forms of anxiety or depression. There are many different causes of anxiety and depression, however it is logical to see that when our children get stuck in the 'down' for long periods, they are not able to experience the joys and highs that life has to offer, and find it harder to get out of the down. Their school work, friendships and interactions with the world suffer and there are many long-term effects.

Currently, 1 in 10 children between the ages of 5 and 16 suffer from a diagnosable mental health disorder and the number of young people aged 15-16 with depression doubled between the 1980s and 2000s. Self-harm and teen suicides are in the increase and by adulthood, 1 in 5 people are diagnosed with anxiety and depression.

While emotional resilience will not be the answer in every case to preventing depression, it will give our children a wider range of skills to deal with mental health issues and act in prevention before it develops into a medical condition. By teaching our children emotional resilience, we are setting them up to deal with stress and adversity in a more rational way.

To foster the development of strong emotional resilience it is important for our children to have strong, connected relationships early – parent to child, sibling to sibling relationships and also a strong community to learn how to communicate and build strong relationships outside of the family. It is also important to teach children about emotions from an early age including emotional intelligence, how to recognize emotions and how to respond to them.

CHAPTER 11

The Importance of Building Relationships: Parent to Child

In the face of major trauma and stress as a child, why are some children able to bounce back and achieve a strong, healthy and productive adulthoods, while others aren't?

The overwhelming difference is the development of a strong, early relationship.

The Center on the Developing Child at Harvard University has found that the key active ingredient to building resilience is the relationship our children has with an adult who cares about them.

Ideally, this relationship is between a parent and a child, although positive outcomes have been achieved through grandparents, school teachers, coaches and other adults who are significant in a child's life.

From these interactive, two-way relationships, children learn how to regulate their behaviour, how to stop crying, defer gratification and develop a tool kit to bring out skills in stressful and challenging situations including focus, self control and planning ahead. As the child gets older, the skills become more sophisticated including being able to monitor situations, solve problems and make good decisions.

In the very early years when developing relationships, children's brains respond to the 'serve and return' interaction that occurs between an adult and a child. When this pattern occurs regularly, it moulds the brain to build key capacities, including self-control and planning ahead and equip children with skills to respond to adversity.

A relationship is effectively the emotional connection we form with others, based on trust and intimacy. Babies are born with a drive to connect with others and as humans we are hard-wired to be social beings with a mission to connect. It is our job as parents to provide the optimum environment to help our children build solid relationships with us, their siblings and people in their community.

How do we build this relationship?

> 'Love is like a precious plant. You can't just accept it and leave it in the cupboard or just think it's going to get on by itself. You've got to keep watering it. You've got to really look after it and nurture it.' ~ JOHN LENNON

We build it on solid foundations right from the very start.

As soon as you start growing a baby in your womb, the natural instincts of a mother kicks in and you and those around you start to build a relationship with your child right from that moment.

From this moment, it is worth thinking about the sort of relationship you want with your child. Talk to your partner about it. Talk to friends about it or write down the characteristics and traits you want to instill in your child and the relationship you want to form. Is it hierarchical? Is it built on respect? Is it a two-way relationship? Is it based on love?

Once your baby is born, the relationship is already forming. How you hold your baby, how you speak to it, how you include it in conversation, the attitude you have around your baby and how you nurture it as a little human being. You are forming a relationship right from this moment that will run for the rest of your lives. The relationship will change and grow through every different stage of development of life and this will be your child's number one example for developing their own relationships later in life.

A baby will connect by gazing into its mother's eyes when she is breastfeeding. From the start, they recognize their mother as the person who picks them up and feeds them, calms them down and learns to trust that they are loved and cared for and it is not until about the age of two or three years that children see themselves as separate to their mother. This baby will know it is loved through its mother's words and touch.

Fathers play a crucial role as well. A baby can hear in the womb from 18 weeks and they know their fathers voice when they enter the world. A father connects with his baby by speaking to it, holding it, cuddling it, changing it's nappy and being there when it cries.

When our first child was born, seeing my husband turn into a father was one of those priceless, magical moments that only happens once in a lifetime. He loved me and cared for me, but seeing him with our tiny little baby in his arms was a whole new level of his being. The connection he formed in those very early days has stayed as strong as ever.

As our children grow and experience life, our relationship changes with them. When they are small, we as parent are their everything and they rely on us for their survival.

By the age of two or three years, when our children are asserting their own independence and need for autonomy, we need to be mindful of the changing relationship. At this age, if we continue to make all the decisions for our children and control every situation, our children will react accordingly. There will be temper tantrums, power struggles and it is hard to manage this behaviour if we don't already have a strong relationship with them. We need to help them explore their world outside of the parent-child relationship to develop their social skills and learn how to navigate their world.

By the time our children are five years old and go off to school, much of the early relationship building has been set and 80 per cent of brain development has occurred. If we have done our job early on, our children will now know how to play with other children on the playground, interact with their teachers and other adults they encounter and deal with some of their own relationship problems. They will also show empathy and compassion towards others.

By the age of 8 or 9 years, our children are really developing their sense of right and wrong and whatever happens from here on in, they will most likely remember for the rest of their lives. Their brain has reached a new milestone and with it comes some added changes in our relationships, both with our girls and boys.

As puberty hits boys around 12 years and girls around 10-11 years, the relationship with our children can change again. As their body changes, insecurity or issues of self-esteem can arise and if we have already built a solid relationship, our children will come to us first to discuss any concerns.

In general, boys form different relationships with their parents than girls do and it is important for parents to keep this in mind when they are building their relationship. Up until the age of 6, a boy is drawn to his mother for social and emotional support. After this age, boys are drawn to their father or father figure to learn the ways of being a boy. It is at this age that fathers or father figures need to step up and build this relationship with their boys. Girls are somewhat more complicated than boys when it comes to relationships. There tends to be more 'emotional baggage' and much more is needed to invoke a spirit of kindness and compassion in their words and thoughts. Developing their positive inner critic becomes key. It's obvious that boys and girls have different interests and develop at different times – both important pieces of knowledge to keep in mind when forming this important, life long relationship.

Micro-Moments of Connection

Unlike building a relationship with an adult, children live in the moment. Kids don't dwell on the past or see further than a few days or, at a stretch, a couple of weeks into the future.

For adults who factor past and present much more into our days, we build a relationship through spending quality periods of time with each other. So we might plan a 'date night' or a weekend away or a night getting intimate 'together'. Often the anticipation for the future event will help to build on the relationship.

But for our kids who live in the moment, we need to join them in this place and build connection in a different way. Rather than planning slabs of 'quality time' that might come around once a week or once a month, we need to build connection through micro moments.

Micro-moments of connection are little snippets of verbal and non-verbal communications between us and our kids that only last a few seconds or a few minutes. The term micro-moments were first coined by parent educator, Maggie Dent who talks about the importance of building a love bridge with our children through these micro-moments of connection.

Some examples of micro-moments you can use with your kids are:

- Make a silly face at your child and they will make it back
- Stand at the door in the morning and give every child a high five on their way out
- Write a little love note to put into their lunch boxes or school bag
- Join them spontaneously on the couch to watch their favourite TV show
- Wink at your kids when they look at you
- Create a symbol for I Love You (for 'I' point to your eye, for 'Love' point to your heart and for 'you' point back to your child) and do it randomly

- Put the radio on in the kitchen and have a spontaneous dance party with your kids for the length of the song
- Make up a little saying that just you and your child understand
- At bedtime, start a ritual with 'I love you higher than the tallest mountain or lowest than the deeper sea'
- Learn their hand clapping games like scissors, paper, rock or tic tac toe and do it with them
- Go into the dress up box and put some accessories on – a wig, cape or tail and pretend it's completely normal when you see your kids
- When their favourite song comes on in the car, crank it up loud and sing it with them
- Pick up and start reading their favourite book at random in the day and they will join you for a snuggle
- Tell them you love them completely out of the blue or start sharing what characteristics you really love about them, just because

DISCIPLINE AND PARENT-TO-CHILD RELATIONSHIPS

> 'Respond to your children with love at their worst moments, their broken moments, their angry moments, their selfish moments, their frustrated moments, their lonely moments, their inconvenient moments... because it's in their most unlovable human moments that they most need to feel loved' ~ L.K KNOST.

It is important to continue to build and develop a loving, respectful relationship with our children when we are disciplining them.

Think of the top 3 ways your children behave that really presses your buttons.

Do they fall under these categories?

- Not doing as asked
- Talking back
- Temper tantrums
- Saying no
- Whining, grizzling
- Morning routines: Not getting out of the house on time
- Bedtime routines: Not going to bed and staying there at night
- Sibling rivalry

At the parenting workshops I run, these are the most common behavioural struggles parents have with their children on a daily basis. Multiply that by two or three children and that is a lot of power struggles and time spent disciplining each day.

So how do you find the balance between discipline and continuing to develop a loving relationship?

There is no firm science on this and it will depend very much on the family and the individual children. It will also be based on the type of parent involved and the situation we are in. There are generally four types of parenting styles and each style will impact on the relationship you develop with your child. The four types of parenting styles are:

1. AUTHORITARIAN PARENTING: Parents set the rules and expect their child will follow. Parents are strict with discipline and their no-negotiation, rigidity in rules often relies on punishment and withdrawal of affection to shape their child's behaviour. While these children will be able to follow the rules throughout life, they will either rebel from their parents later on or be shy and withdrawn with a lack of self-confidence to respond. They can also become aggressive and hostile as they lack the means for a sense of control and autonomy.

2. AUTHORITATIVE PARENTS: Parents set boundaries they expect their kids to follow, however they show respect for the children they are parenting and allow them some exceptions. There is rule setting together as a family and some negotiation and compromise will happen. Parents are responsive to their children and demanding at the same time. They discipline with love and affection and tend to use consequences to enforce behaviour. There is room to express emotions and children tend to grow up to be successful adults who are good at making decision and comfortable expressing their own options.

3. PERMISSIVE PARENTING: Parents are lenient and they only step in when there is a problem. They don't offer too much discipline and there are few consequences for misbehaviour with the mantra that 'kids will be kids'. If any rules do exist, they are inconsistent and kids generally decide the rules and consequences on the fly. These parents are responsive but not demanding and it is often that their kids rule the roost. These children tend to ignore authority, struggle to fit into the education system that affects their academics and are disrespectful and aggressive. They are often creative and spontaneous and depending on their own self-discipline, they often have a happy disposition.

4. DISENGAGED OR UNINVOLVED PARENTS: These parents are neither responsive nor demanding. Children often struggle to get their needs met and there is little consistent discipline. There tends to be few rules and little nurturing or care as to what the children are doing. Children in this category suffer the highest psychological issues, rank lowest in happiness and have frequent behaviour problems.

As you can see, each style has its pros and cons. Parents are either true to the styles, or find their own mix between each of them to raise their kids in the best possible environment.

With that in mind, children most often thrive in an environment where there are solid routines and boundaries, where there is love and respect both ways and where there is enough freedom and autonomy for individual thought as well as guidance to grow and develop. It is ideal to find a parenting style that will allow you to shine as a parent and for your kids to thrive.

So how can you find the right balance to build that strong, loving and connected relationship with your child while still providing boundaries and guidance?

Largely based on the Positive Parenting philosophy of parenting, here are some ideas that can go towards nurturing our relationship with our children, while holding our ground on discipline. It is more aligned to the authoritative parenting style and equips both us and our children with the necessary skills to build a strong relationship.

Before you respond with discipline

Before you start disciplining your child, you need to first be clear on why your child is behaving the way they are in the first place.

If your child has just had a tantrum, what has triggered it?

If they have broken their sisters new toy, why?

If your child has just run across the road without holding your hand, why did they do it?

If your child has just yelled back at you for turning of the television, why did they do it?

Running through the following questions will help you better understand why your child has done what they did and respond accordingly.

- Does your child have an unmet need? Are they tired, hungry, overwhelmed, need more exercise? Have they had too much

screen time or are they feeling unsafe?
- Do they have age appropriate independence, control and autonomy?
- Do they feel a sense of significance with in your family?
- Do they feel a sense of belonging in our family?
- Has a changed occurred recently at home, at school or in their immediate environment? This is any change – a new bed, a new sibling, a change in schools, daycare rooms, a new child in their class at school, a different teacher for the day.

Another significant reason our children behave like this is because their brains are not fully developed to deal with these massive emotions or significant events. In fact the part of the brain that deals with emotions is not formed until the age of 25. So they are largely reacting the way they do because they don't have the same brain capacity we have to think and act rationally. And they have not developed their emotional capacity to deal with the situation.

How to respond with discipline

So how can we respond to these behaviours and still keep our relationships in tact?

1. Be Kind AND Firm.

These two words together are a tautology – kind AND firm is a tricky balance to get right.

Being kind means that, when your child does the wrong thing, you connect with your child before you correct them. You get down to their level. You use a normal voice. Your first reaction isn't to yell, smack or shame. You validate their big feelings. You do a needs check to see why they are behaving like they are.

For example, when your child is having a temper tantrum because you gave them the blue cup instead of the red cup, rather than pull the cup out of their hand and tell them to stop whining – validate their feelings and use touch if they allow you to get them through the temper tantrum or huge outburst of emotion.

But here is the firm bit. When the temper tantrum is over, don't give in and let them have the cup they wanted. Stand firm in giving them the cup you got out.

The firm part is setting the boundaries and rules and being consistent around them. So if your rule is that your child gets whichever cup they are given, then hold fast. When they finish their temper tantrum or even when it is in full swing, don't offer them another colour cup.

However, if your child usually gets a choice here on which colour cup they can have between a red cup and blue cup, and you forgot to give them one so they are now having a temper tantrum, you would need to go back and say, 'Yes sorry, I forgot to ask – Would you like the red cup or the blue cup?'

Another example to demonstrate kind and firm is when you put your child to bed. You set up the routine around bedtime. Make sure there is time in there for a story and cuddles. Put all the habits in there, for example, brush your teeth, go to the toilet, read a story, have a cuddle, lights out. Once you have set up the routine and rules around bedtime – be firm. If the routine doesn't allow your child to come out for a drink, then send them back to bed without a drink. The minute you give them a drink, they will know they can do it again the next night. Make sure they take a drink to bed so they can't use being thirsty as an excuse for getting up.

Being kind and firm can be hard to get the balance just right. It is all about trial and error and what works for one of your children here, might not work for the next so it is being able to adapt your kind and firm to each child. The key ingredients are having robust routines and expectations in place and being consistent with each one.

Another great example is around technology.

Brain researcher and children's technology expert, Dr Kristy Goodwin talks about the techno tantrum.

Our otherwise well-adjusted child has a tantrum when they are told to get off the X-Box or turn the television off. To stop these tantrums, we need to have rules around technology use. It might be that our children know they can watch two programs on television before it is turned off so at the end of the second program, turn the television off. They will soon know that this is the rule and will follow it. With Mindcraft, Dr Goodwin suggests agreeing to turn it off when day turns to night or before your child gets on, find out exactly what they intend to do for that session and turn it off afterwards. It wouldn't be kind to turn it off half way through their session and it is firm to turn it ensure it is turned off at the end of their session as agreed.

2. MAKE A CONNECTION BEFORE CORRECTION.

Our first response to misbehaviour or emotional outbursts should be love, followed by the correction. This can take a lot of patience and knowing how to pause from the parents end and is not always easy to do. The other thing is to not an over-correction. It is best to remind your child of the rules and boundaries at the time and then once the dust settles – maybe the next day when it has been forgotten, talk to your child to find solutions for how they could have behaved differently. For example, when James is in the bath that night, say it wasn't so great to push Johnny over in the sandpit today, was it? What could you have done instead? Or what are some rules around playing nicely together with friends?

3. DO A NEEDS CHECK.

The good news is that our children don't wake up in the morning and deliberately decide to misbehave. They don't set out to make our mornings harder because they won't brush their teeth or forget how to put their shoes on. There is usually a reason – and a very good one at that.

Our children generally have a tantrum or yell back at us because they are trying to meet a need.

At any given point, every human is on a mission to get a need met. Whether it be that they are hungry, need a coffee, need to go to the toilet, need to photocopy a document, need to get to work on time, need to get to a meeting, need to check Facebook – our children are no different. Their needs are just heightened. With their immediacy and irrational nature at this age, they generally want their need fulfilled NOW and sometimes they struggle to even identify their needs so we need to recognize it for them.

When a tantrum unfolds or a fight breaks out or whatever behaviour it is your child is doing that is really pressing your buttons, ask yourself these questions:

- Is my child overtired? Did my child go to bed on time last night? Is it Week 5 of a school term and my child is tired? Has my child started daycare early this week and finished late to fit into with my work schedule? Have we crammed too many other activities into this week and they are now exhausted?
- Is my child hungry? Is it straight after school and your child did not eat their lunch so they are starving? Did they finish their breakfast? Or are they hungry because it is after their usual dinner time?
- Has my child eaten the right foods today? Did they have chocolate and lollies and are now on a sugar high? Have they had the adequate fruit, proteins, carbohydrates and dairy today?
- Has my child had enough exercise today?
- Has my child had too much screen time today and not enough outside time?

- Has my child's routine changed? Was there a new teacher at the school? Have they just moved classrooms at Day Care? Or was there a more permanent change going on?
- Is something going on at school I don't know about?

By understanding the situation and reacting to their needs, it helps to come from a place of acceptance and understanding, rather than a place of aggression or anger.

4. GIVE AGE APPROPRIATE INDEPENDENCE, CONTROL AND AUTONOMY.

From the age of 18 months, or maybe even younger our children start to assert their independence and need for autonomy; this can be a major source of tantrums, misbehaviour and power struggles between a child and their parent.

Many parents feel the need to control the situation. There are a lot of reasons for this. It might be unsafe for a child to do what they want to do, it might be quicker if an adult does it, or less messy or it might even look better if a parent steps in. However, from this young age it is important to set our children up to have control over their own choices.

Ideally, slowly by slowly, we teach our children the skill to be independent and autonomous so when it comes time for them to leave home, they have these skills to go out on their own and lead successful lives. Giving them age appropriate choices and letting the reigns go at the right time of our children's development will help them develop these skills.

1-3 years. In a café recently, a mother was feeding her 10 month old baby mashed potato and pumpkin from a spoon. She had also given the baby food straight on the highchair tray and the baby was happy to eat the food from the highchair. The mother kept trying to shovel the food in from the spoon and the baby was spitting it out, but still happily chewing on the food from the tray. The baby clearly wanted to feed herself. The mother was getting more and more frustrated that she wasn't eating the spoon food. Her mother could have given her daughter the spoon with the food on it or because she was happily eating her finger food, put enough on her tray to fill her up. It is about being creative and meeting our kid's needs at the time.

Another area of choice that can cause power struggles is clothes and dressing. By the age of about two or three years, children will want to dress themselves. This is a classic case of parents needing to let go of image and ego. By the time our kids go to school, we want them to be able to dress themselves independently and get ready for school largely on their own. So when our children want to start to dress themselves at two or three, let them.

My daughter spent most of her time when she was this age in a princess dress. Her Great Aunt ran a costume shop and she would give her the most beautiful princess dresses. Each morning, she would pull one out of the draw and walk down to breakfast in it. And we accepted that is what she would wear. The odd day she didn't wear her princess dress threw my husband. She would come down in a mismatched outfit with clashing colours or stripes and my husband wanted her to match and look well dressed so more often that not, he would send her back up and try to make her change. Undoubtedly an unnecessary power struggle would ensue and there was much exasperation from both sides.

To help children with choosing their own clothes and dressing on their own, sort their clothes into the appropriate draws. For example all the shorts in one draw, t-shirts in another and socks in another so they can easily choose what they want to wear. Also, put clothes in there that YOU want them to wear. If you don't like tracksuit pants, don't put them in the drawer.

Choices at this age should be limited to two or three choices, for example, it might be choosing which plate they want for dinner from a choice of two plates or if they want to have apples or bananas for snack. You don't want to give them too much choice or it can go the opposite way. With too much choice, there is an added level of confusion and it sets children up for tantrums and power struggles. Similarly, give a choice that you are happy with so it makes it easier for you and them.

4-6 years. Children will go to school between the ages of 4 to 6 years and as their mind grows and experiences change, they will want more independence and choice. Remember it must be age appropriate so still limit choices at this age, but broaden what they are choosing.

Choices at this age include:

- Which snack they want in their lunch box
- Choosing the right school shoes or sneakers (out of the choices you are also happy with)
- Choosing how they want their hair done in the morning – plaits, pony tail or a spike
- Which toothpaste they want to use and colour of their toothbrush
- Which television show to watch (that you are happy with) or which app to play on their iPad
- How to use their free time at home
- Which extra curricular activities they want to do (that you are happy with and can get them to)
- If they want to go to a birthday party or not and what present to buy their friend
- Which equipment to play on at the park

We also need to give our children increased independence at this age by increasing their responsibility.

Age appropriate responsibilities are:

- Carrying their own school bag
- Holding the lead when you are walking the dog
- Paying for something at the shop counter
- Putting their own shoes on
- Brushing their own teeth sometimes
- Household chores like setting the table or helping to fold the washing

7-10 years. By this age, children are increasing their responsibility and choices at school and so will be looking for more independence and autonomy at home too.

Think about your childhood at this age. What were you doing? Sadly the freedom we enjoyed has changed – perceived or real safety concerns have come into play and we no longer have the freedom of letting our kids go out on their own as much as we did at this age.

While we increase the choice and responsibility at this age, remember to provide other avenues to increase independence and control. For example, sending your kids outside to play on their own, standing at the park gate to let them play at the park on their own, sitting on the steps at the beach while they play on the sand a safe distance away from you.

This is probably the hardest age to release the reigns but will be worthwhile when they reach the next stage.

Choices at this age include:

- All mentioned in the 4-6 age range with an added level
- How they want to use their birthday money (spend, save, share)
- What extra curricular activities they want to do
- How they spend their time on weekends
- Which friends to have over for playdates or sleep overs
- What they want to read or play (with some rules)

Age appropriate responsibility at this age include:

- Making their own lunch sometimes
- Walking the dog around the block with their friend or sibling
- Buying their own ice cream at the local shop
- Doing homework on their own

By setting the right boundaries and rules around much of these choices, you will give your children more choice and responsibility because they will know your expectations, boundaries and follow the safety rules.

11-14 years. This is the age range where children will really start to push the independence and control boundaries and you will need to know how to respond. Ideally, if you have increased the choice and responsibility appropriately through the ages, by now it will be a natural progression to increase independence to suit their age

Choices at this age include:

- Which subjects to do at school
- What sporting clubs or activities they want to be part of
- How to spend their time at home
- When to complete their homework (with boundaries and habits already set)

Age appropriate responsibility at this age include:

- Getting ready for school including making lunches
- Folding the basket of washing or doing the laundry
- Cleaning the fish tank on their own
- Washing the dog
- Cleaning up the kitchen or unpacking the dishwasher
- Catching the bus home from school on their on

- Going for a bike ride with friends
- Meeting friends at the mall or going to the movies with friends (at the upper limit of this age)

At 14, children could start a simple job, like pamphlet dropping or working in the local newsagency or supermarket.

By allowing our children to have choices and responsibility when they are ready, it reduces many of the power struggles we will have with them and also helps build a sense of trust that is imperative in a healthy relationship. However, this will only work if we set up robust boundaries around these choices and responsibilities and are consistent in our expectations.

5. Develop your child's sense of significance

Following on from allowing our children to develop independence through choice and responsibility, our children want to feel significant.

Wanting to feel significant is a human trait and we all want to feel important or worthy of attention. Because of their egocentric nature, children especially want to know they are worthy and hold a place of significance in the larger family unit. . We all need some power and autonomy of our own to feel good and in control.

Between the age of 2 and 7 children's thoughts and communications are typically about themselves and again as teenagers. They assume that other people see, hear and feel exactly what they do. When the world revolves around just you, you want people to notice you and see you for who you are. That is often why you will hear at the park, 'Look at me, Mummy' a thousand times when your child is three. It is a developmental stage and we need to nurture this stage.

To nurture our child's sense of significance we can do the following:

- Give choice and responsibility – as already outlined, giving age appropriate choice and responsibility is important for promoting independence. However, it is also important for our children to

be recognized for what they can do. Kids love to do 'big people' jobs around the house from a young age because they feel worthy and significant. They will vacuum or sweep the floor because they have been watching you do it and want to capable like an adult.
- Recognise their strengths – once we have identified our children's strengths, recognize them. Use encouraging words to support their efforts and provide them with the opportunity to feel this success or significance
- Let your kids put on shows for you – while it can be tedious sitting and watching your child put on their latest 'concert', you are actually doing them a real favour. You are giving them a sense of significance.
- Don't order, use manners – when you want your child to do something, phrase it with manners. For example, 'Please put your shoes on now' instead of 'get your shoes on now'. No one likes being told what to do all the time and it is easy to fall into the pattern of ordering. Assume your child is your boss at work and see if you would direct them like that – it's reassuring to know you wouldn't tell your boss at work to 'hurry up and go to the toilet'.

When children don't feel significance, they dig their heels in harder to do their own thing and the power struggles ensue. If we give them some choice, responsibility, time to show us who they are and talk instead of always ordering and directing – we will reduce the misbehaviours and need for discipline.

6. Develop your child's sense of belonging

A sense of belonging is a human need. It is right up there with food and shelter.

To really develop a connected relationship with our children and also to minimize many of the hard behaviours they display, we need to develop their sense of belonging to family and to the wider community.

Every human being is hard wired to want to belong. We want to feel like we are part of a something bigger than ourselves and be accepted into the 'group'. The group might be to one or two other people, or it might be to the whole of humanity – or a balance in the middle where people belong to a family, church group or community group. They know they are not alone.

If we don't find our 'group' to belong to, we often falter. Faltering in our children looks like tantrums, sibling fights, talking back or reacting irrationally to a 'normal' situation. Faltering for adults might be feeling withdrawn or having a burning desire to connect and be part of a community that will play out in different physical or mental ways. Loneliness or social isolation is a product of our want and need to belong to a group. When we are connected with others, we experience increased motivation, wellbeing and more enjoyment in life.

Providing a sense of belonging for our children is about providing a loving, nurturing environment where children feel valued, listened to and part of the 'team'. They know their opinion matters and they know we have heard what they say. They feel accepted in the 'group'. This has almost got to be a throw back to our evolution from animals that operate in a pack mentality – we need to be connected to that pack to feel secure and valued.

In the hurry up culture we have created, this is one of the areas that are often overlooked in families. If you are working or running a household it can be hard to take the time to really listen to what our kids are telling us. 'Busy time' fills the gaps of time that we need to dedicate to just being together as families to really connect. This also plays out in classrooms. Children do 'busy work' rather than spending time playing together and interacting as a pack.

Case study: Clara and her mum

It was a busy morning in a household of 6 kids and Clara's mum and dad needed to get everyone out of the house and to work.

They had an 8.15am deadline. The mother does most of the heavy lifting in this house and had already been to swimming with her eldest at 6.30am. She was to be home at 7.45am and the kids were to be ready. She had been at a meeting the night before and it had been a hectic week of dropping kids off and picking them up with little time to sit down and breathe.

The mum walked in the door and it was all looking good, so the dad left and went off to work and all the kids were walking out the door at 8.15am. Little did she know that the dad had not long got out of the shower, had left the kids to get their breakfast and then they watched television. It was off by the time mum got home but he hadn't really even spoken to the kids. Good morning the mum thought.

Her middle daughter Clara had different ideas about the morning. She hadn't seen her mum the night before at all because of the meeting and only for a very short time that morning with her so as they got the front gate, Clara decided she had forgotten her home readers and ice block money and ran back inside. She lingered inside. Her mum was out the front calling to her to hurry up as the others were already walking to school. Clara saw this as the perfect opportunity to spend this time with her mum – even if she was cranky. But mum was focused on getting the kids to school and already running through her work to do list.

When Clara came out of the house, her mum told her she should be more organized in the mornings and started to deliver her rant about mornings and how she should remember everything. Clara mentioned something about the 100 night reading certificate she had gotten at school yesterday – her mum was too busy telling her to hurry up and she didn't acknowledge it. By the time they had walked the short few blocks, it hadn't been a good 10 minutes for either of them and she kissed her daughter and walked out the gate. Her other children were already well inside the gates and at school.

Her daughter ran after her crying saying 'I'm too scared to go to class by myself'.

Two things could have happened here.

1. The mum could have told her to stop being silly and go to class like she had done every other morning. She could have left her little girl crying at the gate to hurried off to get to her first meeting.

Or 2. She could give have given her daughter a cuddle, walked her to class and talked to her on the way about the weekend and what they might do together.

If this mum was to choose number 2, she would need to do a complete shift of her own feelings and thoughts to recognize her little girl wanted her to connect with her this morning and feel that sense of belonging she hadn't been feeling. She didn't see her dad or her mum much this morning, she hadn't seen them much this week and she needed that small window of time to connect.

Thankfully Clara's mum recognized this and walked her to her classroom, gave her a big cuddle, pulled a silly face to lighten the mood and reminded her of the family picnic they had planned for the weekend.

You can see in this example that Clara needed to connect and feel that sense of belonging this morning. She may have forgotten her home readers and ice block money on purpose, but even if she didn't, she lingered inside until the others had left and obviously wanted to spend that time with her mum. She wanted to feel that sense of acceptance and belonging and so told her mum about the certificate she got, but her mum didn't hear.

It is these cues from our kids we can get if we really listen and check in with them to know how they are feeling. To build this sense of belonging for our kids, it requires active effort and practice and being able to recognize the big picture of how we are parenting.

It is easy to get stuck in the parenting trenches like Clara's mum was doing and not look at the week or the needs of Clara when she had her own work needs to meet. But to look at the big picture when our children misbehave and see what is actually going on for them is how we nurture this sense of belonging and continue to build a strong relationship.

Here are some easy ways to create a sense of belonging for your child.

- Don't use time outs for disciplining – by using time outs, we are crushing this sense of belonging. Our children are being singled out from the pack and moved to a place where they no longer belong to the family unit.
- Validate emotions – by accepting our children's emotions and helping them to understand they are real, we are validating them and acknowledging they are important.
- Listen to your children – what doesn't necessarily feel important to you, might feel huge to our children so listen to their words and respond accordingly.
- Don't single out or shame a child in front of others – this can be a subconscious choice, but by singling a child out you are eroding their sense of belonging to the group. They feel embarrassed, ashamed and will probably act out further.
- Find a community – school might be enough for our children to feel a sense of belonging. Sporting clubs and other community groups are also important.

- Set clear routines and expectations around connecting – if your children know that every night you have a family dinner together and this is the time to talk about problems, have fun together or connect in another way, they might be OK to wait until then. If they know that on the weekends, you always go to the local markets together as a family to get a coffee and they feel that acceptance and love, they might wait until then. It is important to set up these fun, family times for connecting and keep your kids in the loop. Be spontaneous for connecting too, but find a routine of family time.
- Be mindful of your language when disciplining. A sense of belonging is created through collaboration as a family, not competition. Be aware that you are not pitting your kids against each other by using sayings like: Comparing one another: 'Well Billy can tie his shoes and he is only 5, you are 7 so why can't you?' or labeling them: 'You are really good at sport, but your brother is better at music'. These comparisons and labels invoke unnecessary competition between kids and don't allow them to be on an equal footing with the family unit.

7. When the lid flips – stop

'When our little people get overwhelmed by big emotions, it's our job to share our calm not join their chaos.' ~ L.K Knost

From the age of about 18 months, children start to develop the prefrontal cortex of their brain. This development continues until their mid-20s when it reaches full development, with development on the full continuum along this time period.

The prefrontal cortex, at the front of our brain behind the forehead, controls our emotions. It is our 'executive' for our decision-making processes and gives us much of our intelligence and problem solving abilities. It is the part that gives us the ability to pause before acting, regulates our empathy, compassion and morals and where our schema is stored or memories of our past and present experiences. It is this part of the brain, for the most part, that helps us make sense of the world and react to it.

Imagine this. Your child is developing their prefrontal cortex right until the age of 25! They are learning how to control their emotions, make good decisions and solve problems. They are learning how to react to certain situations and building up their bank of memories. However, we as parents have a fully developed pre-frontal cortex. We have the capacity to control our own emotions, make rational decisions and find solutions for problems. We know how to react to the world and if we don't we have the capacity to find a way to do it.

Let's relate this to child's behaviour. They are still learning how to be rational – many of their days are spent enacting their still irrational brain to situations. It is our job as parents then to use our rational brain to react to a situation.

If your child has accidently dropped her plate of dinner on the floor, how do you react? How do you react to the spilled milk at the dinner table? How do you react to a full on tantrum in the supermarket? How do you react when your child yells at you?

These are common child behaviours and it is how you use your rational brain to react that can make all the difference when disciplining your children and forming your relationship with them.

Renowned neuropsychiatrist and author, Dr Daniel Siegel has developed a Hand Model of the Brain to show how the prefrontal cortex is integral in controlling the way we parent and the response from our children.

Dr Siegel shows how we 'flip our lid' to expose our irrational brain. Close your hand around your thumb. Hold it up like this. Imagine the hand is your brain with your forehead at the front of your fingers and your wrist if your spine. Your prefrontal cortex is your thumb. Every time you react irrationally to a situation, your fingers lift up and Dr Siegel calls this 'Flipping your lid'. By flipping your lid, you are tapping into the irrational part of the brain that doesn't allow you to use rational thinking to make decisions. Imagine if your child, who is still developing their prefrontal cortex also flips their lid. You will have two flipped lids or two irrational brains trying to make sense of the situation in front of you. Watch Dr Daniel Siegel presenting a Hand Model of the Brain here www.youtube.com/watch?v=DD-lfP1FBFk.

As the parent who has the developed or rational brain, it is our job to close the lid and look at the situation rationally again.

So how do you keep the lid closed?
It is a matter of retraining your brain to react more rationally to the behaviours that really press your buttons, like the temper tantrums, spilling the milk, sibling fighting, talking back or saying no.

The first thing you need to do is be aware of when your lid is going to flip. This will be different for every person. It might be a tingling feeling in the pit of your stomach or your toes curling or your face going red. Also be aware of how you behave when your lid flips – do you yell, smack, shame, restrain or send your kids to another room?

Think about this situation.

CASE STUDY:
COOKING DINNER WITH BEN AND JOSIE

You are in the kitchen preparing dinner and your children, Ben and Josie are playing with play dough on the kitchen table. Everything is going fine until you hear that Ben wants the shape cutter Josie has and she doesn't want to give it up. Next thing you know, Ben slaps his sister on the arm and Josie erupts in shreds of tears and shouts back 'I hate you' and a full blown sibling fight starts.

You can feel your face flushing red, your heart rate has quickened and the anger is literally bubbling up. Both Ben and Josie have done the wrong thing. They clearly don't know how to share even though you have told them and told them and they have also forgotten that hitting is not tolerated.

You can react to the situation two ways here:

1. Your brain flips – you race to the table yell at both the kids, hit Ben for hitting his sister and send Ben to his room. You tell Josie she started it for not sharing and she can also have time out in her room. They leave still shouting at each other and you and you are shouting back at them. They sulk in their rooms and you fume as you finish cutting up the potatoes. It has been 10 minutes since the incident and both you and your children are still feeling angry and upset and it will take some time to calm the house down again.

Or 2. You could pause – know the feelings that are bubbling up inside, breath 10 times and then walk over to the table. In a calm voice state that neither were acting in a nice way and because you have already set the expectations before they started playing with the playdough, you and your child will both know that the consequence for fighting with each other was to pack the play dough away. You tell Ben it was the wrong thing to hit his sister and get him to apologise. You give them both a hug and get them to pack up the play dough. That night when you are bathing Ben, you talk to him about how hitting is sister was wrong and talk together about solutions to react better next time. When you put Josie to bed, you talk to her about the importance of sharing and using her voice to tell Ben he could have it when she had finished cutting out the shape.

If you went down path 1, you flipped your lid. Your kids also flipped their lids. Everyone was angry and the situation was prolonged. You didn't use the teachable moment to teach that hitting was not OK and neither did you teach about sharing. You kept on yelling and the situation got worse. It took much longer to calm the house down and you had to pack up the play dough yourself.

So what can you do if you have two flipped lids – both you and your child have flipped lids?

Take control of the situation. React with love and connect before you correct. Calm the situation down. Talk to your child and reassure them they are in a safe, caring environment. And STOP. You need to stop first – you need to stop yelling or whatever reaction you have had to first so your child also stops. Watch how quickly you stopping can stop a power struggle. Validate that you have both flipped your lids and look at the toolbox you have developed.

It is our job as the parent to keep our lid shut and if it does open, stop it as quickly as possible. Remember our children's brains are still developing their rational capacity and so we need to take control of the situation and STOP. Don't keep fighting, don't keep yelling, just stop and bring back the calm and rational brain.

8. KEEP CALM WHEN YOUR KIDS ARE PRESSING YOUR BUTTONS

How do you keep your calm when your kids are pressing your buttons? It is hard. At the parenting workshops I run, the first question parents always asked is 'But how?'.

Firstly, you need to be in check with your own emotions and know when you are going to flip your lid.

Then you need to have a toolbox of ideas to help yourself stay calm. Here are some ideas:

SHORT-TERM SOLUTIONS
- Have some self time out (don't put your child in time out, put you in time out!).

- Walk into the next room to take a few deep breaths
- If you are in the car, get out of the car and walk around it
- Take a quick walk in the garden
- Do some vacuuming – there is something great about the noise of the vacuum to override the noise of your house
- Develop a breathing routine you can do in the presence of your kids
- Go to the toilet and shut the door to give yourself a few seconds to calm down and react rationally – one of my friends put herself in the pantry for a couple of minutes to have this space
- Hang out the washing

LONGER-TERM SOLUTIONS

If you are in a pattern of yelling or reacting to a situation irrationally, it will take time to break the pattern. It is really important to give yourself the time to break the pattern and know that sometimes you will still react irrationally and that is OK. To start, focus on the 80/20 principle – if you strive to do it 80 per cent of the time, the other 20 per cent of the time it is OK to slip and revert back to your old way. Don't be too hard on yourself as you are only human. Set yourself a daily goal and acknowledge every time you react rationally to a situation.

To react rationally, you need to be at your optimum. Often times when you are tired, run down, working too hard, not getting enough time with your kids or juggling too many balls in the air, you will react irrationally. It's important then that you have had enough sleep, are eating well and find the right balance between time with your kids and time away from your kids. Have some good self-care techniques in place to help you find this balance – maybe have a massage, do a work out, have a pedicure, coffee with a friend or go for a run/walk to fill the 'mummy cup of love'. When the cup is full, it is easier to react from a rational place, rather than an irrational place.

You also need a toolbox of ways to deal with these that could include:

- Having clear boundaries, routines and expectations in place
- Teaching your child to recognize their own emotions and have strategies to deal with anger, disappointment and interactions with others
- Building solid, connected relationships
- Having family fun times together
- Developing a community
- Finding a sense of belonging and significance for your child
- Building resilience through a strong mind, brave heart and healthy body
- Developing a strong set of values, morals and beliefs

As you can see, many of these solutions are long-term and have an equal and opposite effect on each other. For example, if you build a strong relationship, you will have less behaviour problems and if you have less behaviour problems, you will build a stronger relationship.

9. What doesn't work to build a relationship when responding to behaviours?

'Parenting doesn't have to be 'us versus them'. It can be win-win.'
ALISON SMITH.

The way we react when our children misbehave has a major impact on our relationship with our children. It is inevitable that our children will do the wrong thing. Some children will misbehave more than others, but it is the way we react as parents that can harm our relationship. Time outs, smacking, shaming, yelling, revoking privileges and rewards and bribes as reactions to our children's behaviors harm our relationships and here's why.

TIME OUTS. Time outs don't work to build our relationships with our children. It came into 'vogue' as the new way to discipline our children. 'Super Nanny' style children were being banished to their rooms or put on the 'naughty step' to calm down.

However, we already know that our children are incapable of always making rational decisions and the misbehaviour that has just occurred is an outpouring of emotions.

Imagine this: Two year old, Hannah was happily sitting on the floor with her younger brother, Billy building block towers. Billy, at age 11 months crawled over and knocked the block tower down. After Hannah's huge effort to place each block delicately on to the next block and establish her pattern, the block tower was now all over the floor. Her first reaction is to scream, throw herself on the floor and go into full meltdown, tantrum mode. She then takes a swipe at Billy and he is also crying. It sounds like World War 3 has just broken out. While Hannah is going through this huge emotional outburst, you pick her up (against her will) and send her to time out to think about her actions. Her time out spot is in the hallway on the second step and you tell her to sit there for 5 minutes and think about what she has done. You look around after a minute and she is climbing the stairs and so you bring her down and put her back on the step. This happens again and again until you are now in a power struggle with Hannah.

Let's look at this situation more closely. For a start, Hannah is reacting to Billy knocking down her tower – she is disappointed and angry and shows her emotions by having a tantrum and hitting Billy. She doesn't know another way to deal with her disappointment and anger yet because she is only 2. The she is put out of the room – she has been excluded from the situation and her sense of belonging to the group has gone right down. She no longer feels like she is in a safe environment. You have put her there to think about what she has done – but we know at two children have no rational or logical thinking.

Hannah needs to be coached to get through these emotions. And then by checking on her and putting her back on the step – you have just started a power struggle between you and her. It is now a battle between your two year old and you and your patience is probably wearing thin. At the end of the power struggle, she still doesn't know how to deal with her emotions, she thinks running up the stairs will attract your attention even if it were bad attention and she is none the wiser about what she should have done in this situation. She also thinks that because you are holding your 11 month old to sooth him, he is getting all the attention and not her.

Here is an alternative: Billy knocks over the block tower. Hannah has a tantrum and hits Billy. Either you needed to anticipate this was going to happen and move Billy away in the first place or when it happens, make the connection before correction. Go in, cuddle both and validate to Hannah that she would be feeling disappointed and angry because she had put a lot of work into it. Explain that Billy is too young to understand and hitting Billy wasn't the right thing to do. Help her rebuild the block tower with Billy's help. Depending on the mood in the house, it might be the second time your daughter has done this and she really needs some time to calm down, so you could already have a place set up in the room that signals a chill out area or calm down area. This space might be a soft cushion with her favourite books and teddy bears on, or it might be a corner where she can listen to her music. This way she is still with you, you have shown her there is a consequence for her action and all the while you validate her feelings. Later on in the bath that night, talk to Hannah about what she could have done differently if Billy knocked over her block tower rather than hitting him.

This approach also works well for school aged children and you, as the parent will know what works for each individual child. When my eldest daughter was younger, she needed her own space and would react badly if she became overwhelmed. She had an iPod with her choice of music on it and could retreat to a quiet space and listen to it until she had calmed down. She is now 10 and has self-regulated her behaviour to know when she has had enough with the other kids. She will retreat to me or to a quiet space with her music. Over the time, we have tried many different strategies to find her calm down activities or space. Sometimes it is just breathing for her while counting to ten to calm down.

Ideally, you want to help and coach your children to find their own method of calming down. When it becomes intrinsic, they will be able to use it in any situation. Time outs don't help children self regulate their behaviour – rather escalates it with a punishment and usually a power struggle between our children and us.

10 Alternatives to Time Out
- Take a 5-minute break, together
- Give a second chance or another solution
- Have a cuddle
- Read a story together
- Listen to a song
- Pick some flowers together
- Go for a walk together
- Try a breathing exercise
- Spend some one on one time to reconnect the sense of belonging
- Create a chill out space in a central place in the house

Harsh punishments

> *'What you do speaks so loudly that I cannot hear what you say'*
> ~ Ralph Waldo Emerson

Harsh punishments don't work. This is a similar principle to why timeouts don't work. By smacking, yelling or shaming a child, you are not allowing your child to self regulate their own behaviours or emotions, rather punishing them for having these strong emotions and not knowing yet how to deal with them. You are also realigning the relationship to being authoritarian with you in complete control – no one likes to be controlled.

Smacking, yelling and shaming are all punishments that are counterproductive to building strong relationships because of the way you make that child feel. It is easy to slip into using these punishments as a quick reaction to stop the behaviour, however at the same time it is not building a trusting, loving relationship or allowing us to be the role model we want our children to grow up with.

By yelling or smacking our children, we are showing them it is OK to yell and smack when they get angry. And so the vicious circle begins. When you yell or smack, your children will think it is normal behaviour to do the same and they will lash out or yell back at you. Then you will tell them not to yell or smack and a full-blown power struggle ensues.

Shaming is the lowest form of punishment here because it affects our child's psychological well-being and can have lasting consequence. It erodes their inner self-esteem and self-confidence – the major factors that allow our children to be resilient. It also shapes their inner critic with negative words and feelings that they are not good enough or they are stupid or what ever it is you say often enough to your child's thought pattern.

When you shame a child, you are attacking the child's identity directly, rather than reacting to their behaviour. The key point to remember when your child misbehaves is that it is not the child you need to change, it is the behaviour. It doesn't say what the child did was bad; it says that the child is bad. There is a fine line here and when you cross it, it can have devastating, life long emotional effects on our kids.

Alternatives to punishments

Set clear boundaries and expectations. It is our job as parents to set the rules. We need to be clear in what we want from our children from the start. For example, if one of your rules is your child doesn't jump on the couch; tell them it is wrong to jump on the couch. Keep reminding your children about the rules and expectations, be firm in telling them.

Be consistent. It is imperative that once you have set the rules and boundaries to be consistent around them. For example, if you set a rule that screen time is limited to Friday afternoons and then let them have it on a Tuesday afternoon, you are sending mixed messages. Only let them have screen time on Friday afternoons if that is your rule.

Teach your child how to react to their emotions. Many of our child's misbehaviours happen because they haven't developed their rational decision making processes yet and so are irrational and emotional when reacting to situations. We can help them understand their emotions by validating them, coaching them to find alternatives to bounce back from the negative emotions and provide ways to be positive with hope and optimism.

Rewards or bribes

Here's the sad news – that well meaning star chart on your fridge to get your children to eat their vegetables or clean up the playroom is not working. Well, for the long term anyway.

A bribe is something we offer our children before the event occurs. For example, if you use the toilet, you can have a jellybean. A reward is something we give after the event. For example, if you eat the broccoli on your plate, you get a golden star on your chart and if you eat it five nights in a row, you will get a new toy.

Here's why rewards and bribes don't work.

REWARDS AND BRIBES DO NOT CREATE INTRINSIC BEHAVIOR. Our children are only doing something when we bribe or reward because there is something in it for them. They are not doing it because of the intrinsic value. For example, they are not learning the importance of going to the toilet or that eating their vegetables will make them strong and healthy, but are doing them because they will get a treat from us or miss out on dessert. This is the same when rewards are used in education – it creates finishes, not learners. 'If you are the first to finish, you will get table points'. So the kids rush their work and finish quickly, however to do learn from what they have done. They are only finishing the work for that period.

THEY WILL EXPECT REWARDS FOR THE WORK THEY ARE MEANT TO BE DOING. When we constantly reward our children for doing the washing up or contributing to the running of a household, they come to expect the reward and when it is no longer there or changes in nature, they will want something different.

THEY ARE SHORT LIVED. The star chart might work for a short period to get the playroom clean but will only be a phase. Children loose interest in it quickly and then how will you get them to clean the playroom or to eat their vegetables? It is much easier to show the benefits, rather than reward the behaviour.

IT CREATES A 'WHAT'S IN IT FOR ME?' VIEW. If there are constant bribes and rewards, children are always looking for the next way to get something. What they already have is not enough and so it creates a sense of entitlement – the opposite to gratitude.

CHILDREN LIVE IN THE MOMENT. We forget that children live for the moment they are in. So using bribes like 'If you get out of the house every morning this week, we will go to the beach at the end' doesn't work. They are not thinking of the beach when they are getting ready in the morning, like an adult might be. They are thinking about getting out of the house or what their favourite book is, about school that day or something very shiny and immediate. They don't live in the future or in the past, but for the moment and so long term rewards loose impact quickly and don't meet them where they are.

By rewarding and bribing our children, we are creating a relationship of manipulation and control. If you do this for me, I will do this for you. If you eat everything on your plate, you can have dessert. If you don't hit your brother for a week, we will go to the movies. Children will follow our lead and become very good at manipulating their situations at school or in other social situations where it is not an appropriate way to behave.

On a recent holiday, I was standing knee deep in the surf at the beach watching my three children catching waves on their body boards. There was a mum next to me and we got talking about how life had changed and we were no longer lounging around in the water or sunning ourselves at the beach but frantically watching our little ones catch waves and hope they would pop up again after being dumped for the umpteenth time. After an hour or so, I told my kids that we were getting out after two more waves. The mum next to me was astonished and said she was entirely jealous my kids would listen and actually get out. She said she was already bribing hers with ice cream, lunch out at a café and was about to say they could go on their X-Box for the afternoon. I promised her my boundaries didn't work every time but mostly my kids knew the deal when I said it was time to get out and they did.

Alternatives to rewards and bribes

Set clear boundaries and expectations. When your children know the rules and what you expect from you, they will know it is right to eat their vegetables or get out of the water or do what you have set up and been consistent with.

SET GOOD HABITS. We are all creatures of habit. If we want our children to be out of the house by 7.30am, teach them the steps that need to be completed before they leave the house and it will become a habit. They will know the order of events and follow it without the rewards and bribes because it is intrinsic. It might be that together you draw up a chart of the order of things to do and they follow it each morning until they remember it.

TALK TO YOUR CHILD. Whatever it is you usually reward or bribe your kids for, instead talk to them about why it is important for them to do that activity or have that behaviour. For example, if you are rewarding them for folding the washing, talk to your children about why you need to wash clothes (personal hygiene and appearance) and why they need to be folded (to find the clothes easily in the draw). Or if your chart is to reward them for not hitting their sister for a week, talk to them about why it is important to not hit (it hurts the other person) and coach them with alternatives to hitting (take 10 deep breaths, walk away).

10. MUMS (MOTHER FIGURE) AND DADS (FATHER FIGURE) PLAY KEY ROLES IN RELATIONSHIPS

Both a mum (interchangeable with mother figure) and a dad (interchangeable with father figure) play a crucial role in a child's life. Boys and girls do well when they have both to develop strong, healthy relationships.

If you are a single parent and your child doesn't have the opportunity to see their mum or dad, your children will benefit just as well with a positive role model of the opposite sex in their life. Boys need positive role models to know how to act and be a man and girls need positive female role models to learn how to be a woman. It might be a friend, neighbour, grandparent, aunty or uncle or someone that is around often enough to take a keen interest in your child's life.

A mother (or female role model) helps their girls understand puberty, how to love and be respected by their partner, how to act in social situations, about self-esteem and confidence and the intricate details of how a woman. A father teaches their daughter what to look for a in a man, how to love a man or partner and how to be an independent, confident women. Involved, loving fathers also show their daughters how men should treat a girl, with love and respect. Girls with involved fathers reach their puberty later as well as have less mental health problems later in life.

Mothers help their boys to have empathy and compassion and also how to love. They teach them how to interact respectfully with women and how to show their emotions and care. Boys rely heavily on their mums until the age of 6 to be their carers and providers of love, discipline and respect and then the balance switches to dads. They need their dads to be their role models and show them how to be men, especially in adolescence and through puberty. A loving involved dad tells their boys they matter, that they love them and are proud of what they do. An involved father positive influences his son's social, emotional and cognitive development from a young age.

In traditional families, often the father was the dominant force, his word was final and unquestioned and his influence dominated in all matters relating to the family. Essentially, he was the provider and the mother was the caretaker. It was thought the father didn't play a role in the growth and development of his children until the pendulum started to swing in the 1970s.

When I was born in 1978, my dad was not allowed to come into the birth room and was even sent away until I was born. After a day long, tricky labour, I was born and they called my father who had left the hospital to come back as he now had a daughter. This is in complete juxtaposition to when I gave birth to my own children and my husband was with me for the whole labour and was even fortunate enough to deliver my son with the midwife standing by. This significant shift has had an impact on how a father and child has bonded and the role a father now plays in raising a confident, resilient child both physically and emotionally. Studies now show that children with an involved father are more likely to be emotionally secure, be confident to explore their surroundings, and as they grow older have better social connections. They also play a crucial role in the cognitive development and behaviour of their children.

When both parents/role models are actively involved with building a solid, loving relationship with their children, they have a complete base to explore challenges and issues and bounce back from setbacks and adversity.

The key ingredients to building a relationship with your child are:

- Spending time together
- Giving lots of love, kindness & compassionate
- Being a parent, not a best friend
- Meeting them on their level in the moment
- Giving them space to develop and grow
- Loving and accepting them for who they are, not who you want them to be
- Building micro moments of connection into your every day
- Having fun together often
- Allowing respect to flow both ways
- Helping them feel significance and belonging to the family unit
- Listening – being there for big and small problems
- Disciplining in a positive way
- Taking an interest in their schooling and friendships
- Making it easy for them to be who they are
- Having fun!

CHAPTER 12

The importance of building relationships: Siblings

Strong, healthy relationships with an adult (or parent) are key to developing emotional resilience, however sibling relationships are also very important.

It is often the case that our sibling is our very first peer relationship and they are a breeding ground for learning how to navigate conflict, share resources and have a greater understanding for others. It is probably also going to be one of the longest relationships we will ever have. Friends come and go, but siblings are always going to be there.

It is important then that right from the start of our first meeting with our sibling, there is a positive bond. We need to teach our children to love each other. Their relationship needs to be nurtured and allowed to develop with support from the parents throughout the childhood years to develop into positive, healthy relationships later on. It is not a set and forget once the baby comes home, but a constant teaching of how to nurture the bond and changes as children grow together.

If you have only one child, you can apply the same principles here of early bonding with siblings to cousins, friends or neighbours. It is really important to form healthy habits around building relationships early and so there needs to be some avenue to learn to do this.

During pregnancy

When you are pregnant with your second or subsequent child, the language you use around your pregnancy with your first child is important to start that early bond. Ideally, this will be a joyous occasion and you will share this with your child.

It is sometimes difficult to prepare a toddler for the birth of their sibling because it is such an abstract concept of a growing baby in your tummy. The best way is to involve them as much as possible and educate them about it. Let them feel the kicks. Let them listen to the heartbeats. If they are old enough, they could come to the ultrasound with you and see it on the screen. Show pictures of newborns or let them meet a friend's newborn baby. In the final throes of pregnancy, talk about where you will have the baby and who will look after your child while you are in hospital. Be conscious of using positive language around bringing your baby home.

The birth of a sibling

The birth can be a traumatic experience. You will want to do the best for your first child (or subsequent children) around the arrival of their sibling. This might be to have them completely away from the birth and let them meet the baby when it is born or have them there for the whole experience. This will depend on the age of your child and how you think it will affect their relationship with you and the baby.

A few families I know who had water births at home had their older children at the birth to observe the whole process. Personally, I gave birth to my children in the hospital at the birth suite and left my older children at home asleep in their beds with my lovely friends. It was more important for my then four and two year old to have the routine of the day and not see me in labour, than it was to have them in the room. This is very much a personal choice and it will depend on your child and family construct.

BRINGING BABY HOME

Now this is where the real bond starts. Right from when you bring your baby home, you are starting a life long sibling relationship. Think about the beginning of any new relationship. Your children need to bond.

Here are some ideas to help your children bond:

- Let your child hold your new baby (with your support if they are young)
- Involve your child in the bath or let them help you choose the baby's clothes.
- Limit visitors – spend this beautiful time bonding with your immediate family. Visitors have lots of time to meet your child, but you will be busy letting everyone build a new relationship.
- If your child is feeling some overwhelm or jealously, validate their feelings. It is OK to feel like this as it is something new and once they get used to having a new person in the house, they will accept this is the new situation.
- If you have a toddler and newborn, feeding can be tricky. Make sure your older child has something to do – a snack bag, watching a movie, singing songs with you, reading stories or put yourselves all in the same room and get out the toys. You want to make sure your child is safe and feeling a sense of belonging while you are feeding.
- Try to keep your older child's routine the same as much as possible. Try to do bath, dinner and bedtime at the same time.
- And remember to do whatever works best for you to get through the tiny newborn stage of having a new baby.

WHEN BABY STARTS TO CRAWL

This is often the undoing of the relaxed relationship between siblings and the start of real interaction. Once your baby can crawl, it can interfere with your older child's toys and books. Up until now, the baby has lay in the cot, lay on the floor or been held. Now it can get around, the baby can knock down block towers, move toys and generally create havoc – or so it seems from your older child's point of view.

You need to prepare your older child for what is about to happen and encourage them to move their important things up and out of reach of the baby and then help them to learn to share. This is a whole new stage. Depending on the relationship already and the age of the first sibling, sharing might be fine or it might just tip your little one over the edge and you will hear a lot of 'mine'.

Validate your child's feelings and nurture them through this period. These two are going to need to learn to share as they go through life and this is just the very beginning.

Sibling conflict

As children grow and get into each other's space, they will have disagreements or sometimes even full blown fights. It is our reaction to these as parents that can nurture their relationship, or destroy it.

The reality is that all siblings will have their disagreements. The closer they are in age and the closer they are in proximity to each other through out the day, generally the more they will fight. This can be the bane of many parents' existence and, if they have multiple children, being the referee can be tiring.

However, it is actually OK for kids to have these conflicts (within boundaries) and here is why.

Kids live completely in the moment. They might fight over who gets the red cup and who gets the blue cup and to use it sounds like World War 3 but within minutes – if not seconds, they have forgotten about the colour of the cup and are happily drinking their milk together.

If your kids are close in age (I had three kids in just over 4 years) they will be in each other's space – constantly. They will be playing with the same toys, wanting to get on the same swing, bathing together, eating together, and watching television together, all trying to sit on your knee together. And when they are in each other's space, they are like little lion cubs and need to lash out every now and again.

Kids are territorial. Just like an animal instinct, if something belongs to them, it is 'mine' not 'yours'. So if someone touches your stuff, you will react accordingly. Probably 50 per cent of the fights in our house are because someone has something of someone else's: it could be the lid of their Texta but it was theirs and they don't want anyone else to have it.

It is our job as parents to set up a positive home environment so they can learn valuable lessons from this conflict.

Sibling conflict…
….Builds emotional intelligence. Children learn about relating their own emotions and how they can affect the emotions of others.

….Builds resilience. Children are learning the problem solving skills to bounce back after a fight with another sibling

….Forms the basis of future relationships from a young age. Learning how to navigate a relationship is tricky at any age and by engaging in simple conflict at a young age in a safe environment, our kids learn the necessary skills to engage in other conflicts on the school playground or later in life. It also builds social skills.

Here is the catch – our children are only going to learn all these skills if we coach them along the way and set the boundaries and expectations around conflict.

Firstly, we need to leave them for a certain time to have their argument. We can't jump in too soon or we have wasted an entire learning opportunity. When they have stepped over the rules we already have in place, we then intercept. We then get involved and talk through the situation.

Secondly, we need to teach our children strategies to solve conflict such as taking time out, talking it out, apologizing, creating a pattern interrupt and assessing the emotions of others and ourselves. We do this by talking to our children after a conflict, e.g. 24 hours after when it has all died down and they can be rational again. Also teach them how to negotiate and compromise or give and take to find a resolution.

Thirdly, be mindful of the language you use around coaching or stopping the argument. If you take sides or are always blaming one child, you can be impacting on the creation of a negative relationship and singling out one child against the others. This is where unhealthy competition also arises.

If the conflict is getting out of control, here are a few things you can do to calm it down.

Create a pattern interrupt. If your children are going at it hammer and tong, change the situation. It might be to pack everyone up and take them to the park. Or bring a new toy into the mix. Distract them with lunch (or other food) or a different conversation.

Check if your children's needs are being met. Are they hungry, overtired, thirsty, exhausted, over stimulated, had too much screen time, not had enough exercise that day, been doing too much in their day or emotionally spent or are we giving them too many instructions to get out of the house in the morning? All of these can contribute to your kids being irritable with each other and once their needs a met, the house will again calm down.

Provide opportunities to have fun. Life can get too serious for our kids. If we are running from our job, to school pick up, home to cook dinner and stressed about the washing, finances or whatever it is – it is easy to slip into the everyday of life. Kids need to have fun, so lighten it up. Take them to the park. Pull funny faces. Put the music on and have a dance session. Look back over old photos as a slide show on the computer. Say YES to their requests to have ice cream after school or to go to the park.

Validate emotions, but don't fix. During or after conflict, it is important to validate each person's emotions, but don't try to fix them straight away. Agree it can feel bad after you fight with someone but allow your children time to develop their own strategies to fix the situation. (Then talk about it 24 hours later to give further strategies and support when needed).

When is sibling conflict bad?

When it becomes physical. We have a rule in our house 'No hurting self, No hurting others, No hurting property'. Even in the heat of the moment, this needs to be observed. If there is any sort of physical aggression in sibling rivalry it needs to stop right away as it can play out on the playground and in later life. Again it is about setting the clear rules and expectations around conflict.

When a victim/bully situation occurs. The definition of a bully is when there is a prolonged attack from one person (bully) on another person (victim). It has to be ongoing and harmful. If this happens in siblings, this is also bad. Setting up these sorts of behaviours is harmful to relationship building later in life and can even lead to ongoing learning difficulties and mental health issues.

When it becomes rivalry. If your kids are competing against each other for your time or attention or when the conflict becomes genuine competition for love or affection, this is bad. Look at how it got to this stage and work out ways to pull it out of the rivalry and back into the simple conflict.

When a fight is physical or a child is bullied, it erodes the sibling relationship because there is an issue of not feeling safe in the family surrounds and a poor sense of belonging and significance.

Giving your kids the skills to deal with conflict early on in a safe and positive environment will help them develop strong and healthy relationships later on. And if you help them nurture their sibling relationships, they have an emotional and physical support network to help them bounce back from adverse situations for life.

Ways to encourage positive sibling relationships

Encourage siblings to spend time together. When they are young, send them outside to explore together. When they are older, encourage them to go to the movies together or do a sport together. When they are much older, they could go on a trip together. Try not to fall in the trap of making the eldest responsible for the youngest because their friendship needs to come first and ideally they form as an even relationships – not one with authority and control.

Encourage and model healthy communications between each other. The way you speak to your partner will have a direct impact on the way your kids speak to each other, so model good communication. How often have you heard your eldest child speak to the other children the way you speak to them? By modeling the way we speak to each other in a family, it will have a positive impact for the way they speak to each other.

Do fun things together. By allowing your kids to have fun together and as a family, you are constantly building positive relationships for your kids and strengthening the bond.

Let siblings rely on each other. Find moments or activities where they need to rely on each other. They will need to be age appropriate, but might be as simple as the eldest changing the home readers with the youngest or if one of them loses their hat at school, they all need to work together to find it. Or simply bake a cake together where one person is responsible for breaking the eggs, one for mixing and one for putting it in the oven.

Evoke and encourage empathy. If your child is sick or showing big emotions about something, talk to the other kids to evoke empathy towards the other. If they have empathy, they are more likely to build a solid relationship that is ongoing with each other because they will genuinely care about each other.

Give everyone a chance to speak. Have opportunities in the family where everyone is heard and feels listened to. The dinner table is a great place when you are all together to go around the table and give everyone a turn at saying the favourite part of their day or each person having input into the next family holiday. It is important for each sibling to feel equal so the relationship that is forming is not one sided, but equal from the start.

Be mindful of your actions and language towards each child. If you are favouring one child over another or if you are singling out one of your children constantly, the other siblings will pick up on this and do the same. This can develop unhealthy habits when forming an equal relationship.

Explain the difference between fair and equal. If someone gets a new pair of shoes, do they all get them? No. Explain that fairness is that someone gets what they need at the time and needs vary greatly between children. Just make sure that one child is not getting new shoes all the time and the others are missing out. You need to model fair and equal also.

CHAPTER 13

The importance of building relationships: A Strong Community

Developing relationships in the family, with parents and siblings, are key to having the emotional and physical support networks to help you bounce back from adverse situations.

Relationships in the community also play an important role and to give our children the skills to build their own community is imperative. With their own community, they will have friends, peers, mentors and other adults to seek counsel in difficult times and rely on to bounce back.

The first real community children experience is their school. It is here that we need to nurture and encourage the way our children build friendships. This doesn't mean that you need to go in and push them into every friendship in class, but get involved with the activities that are coming up, be interested who your children played with today and talk to them about strategies to make and keep friends.

My children are Defence Force kids and have moved to five different schools in their short primary school life. To be able to adapt to the changes, our mission was to create a community around ourselves no matter where we lived. The kids had friends to meet, peers to interact with and people to go to that they knew. We lived in

America for two years and it quickly became apparent that the community was very strong in our area and so we joined it. There were 20 kids in our cul-de-sac and every afternoon they were out playing with each other in someone's yard. Other places have not been as welcoming, so we have had to work harder to form the community at sporting groups, at the school or in our park.

For one of my son's school projects, he had to draw his hand and write about the people he trusted on the inside and outside from the people in his community. He wrote his family and friends on the inside and on the outside one of his go to people was the lollipop man at the school gate who stopped the cars while the kids went across the crossing. We saw him most days and had a chat to him. He was obviously a safe face and part of my son's community. The other person that was a surprise was my husband's best friend. We don't see him as often as we like and I doubt he would even know that he is in my son's circle of trust. However, he is part of my son's community to look up to and role model from. Our children will form their community from the people around them and if you ask them it may surprise you who they have in it right now.

Children are hard-wired social beings – in fact all humans are. Unlike adults, they mostly view the world as a safe place and are generally comfortable to meet and talk to new people. We need to encourage this as much as we can. We have fallen into a culture where we teach our kids excessively about stranger danger and we are on high alert that there is an axe murder on every corner. Is this really the case? As a society as a result we are retreating into our homes. We no longer go out of our own way to form our community and yet our children need this extended community to bounce back. They need to find their safe place and space to be able to talk to people and interact. It is our job as parents to role model how to build a community and encourage it. It is easier to parent, easier to be a kid and easier to be a family when you know you are not doing the journey alone.

7 Ways to Build Your Community

1. Get involved. If you are new to a school or preschool, volunteer to do the school fete or the school working bee. Meet the parents. Go to the netball or soccer games and presentations and talk to the parents. Or even be the coach. Do reading at school to get to know your kids friends. Find other community outlets like the local clubs or church.

2. Invite people to your house. Play dates and sleepovers are great ways to get to know your kid's friends and their parents. Invite someone new over to your house for dinner. Have your friends over for a BBQ or dinner regularly.

3. Join a group with other families. Sporting groups are a great place to look to find community. If you are into sailing, join the local Yacht Club. Or join the soccer club or kids sporting club. Many people find their community in church groups. There are plenty of groups around if you look out for them. If you have a dog, there are plenty of dog walking groups around to join as a family.

4. Go to the local park. Parks are still havens for kids to go play and you will meet the local families there. You might have to go six times before you start recognizing anyone but this is a great place to meet people. Swimming pools are also a great place to meet other families.

5. Go to local events. Most areas have a local Christmas concert where you can bring a picnic and rug and be part of the festivities. Or there might be a local market on the weekend near you where families will go. Being part of the local community is a great way to immerse yourself in it.

6. Get off your iPhone. When you are at your kids sporting events or swimming lessons, get off your iPhone. Talk to the parent next to you. They may be far more interesting than what is going on in your phone! Even at the park, don't use it as a time to check your messages, push your kids on the swing and talk to the mum who is doing the same.

7. Stay in touch. When you move schools, houses or towns, stay in touch with your last community because you never know when you will be back. Kids also remember their old friends and it is important to keep in touch because their friendships are intense when they are happening – staying in touch can ease the sense of loss. Social media has made it much easier to stay in touch when you relocate and use it to your family's advantage.

Why is community so important?

By building a robust community for your kids, they feel a sense of belonging to a group. Children thrive when they are with others and know they are part of something bigger than themselves or their family.

It also allows them to have a bigger network to discuss problems they might be having with friends or at school. If your children don't feel like they can come to you to talk about a particular problem, they need someone other than a peer to talk to. It might be your best friend or an adult at school they have formed a relationship with. Having a community allows them to find these adult mentors.

By exposing children to different situations and groups, they learn invaluable relationship skills. By doing this, they learn how to build friendships and keep them and resolve any conflict that might come up.

Being with others is fun. By having play dates or kids over at your house, your children are having a great time. They are being kids. Send them outside to climb trees or play in the yard if space permits and give them time away from direct parent supervision so they can create and imagine their own games. Kids need this time to feel in control and negotiate the games and rules of the games they are playing with other kids without parental input.

Community also takes us out of our little bubble and puts us in a much larger bubble to show us that we are not alone on our journey. Once we get outside our own heads and into the world of others, problems slip away for that time or worries are in the back of our mind. It is the same for children. When they are having fun with others, they have time to forget about anything that is going on for them and just 'be'.

Creating a non-judgmental community

A strong community exists when there is a true sense of belonging and a collective goal or purpose. For two years, I worked as the Public Relations Manager at a shelter for the homeless, The Wayside Chapel in the heart of Sydney's Kings Cross district. The mission was to create a community with 'no us and them'. There was no judgment or barriers to people who had mostly outstayed their welcome in every other community and who were some of the most disadvantaged people in Australia. They were mentally ill, drug addicted, homeless, poverty stricken, socially isolated and had mostly been shunned by society because of their choices in life. However, Wayside opened its arms and provided a place where these people could 'be'. It grew into a community centre where people from all walks of life would come to Wayside to connect with the community. No one was turned away and this is what a true community is – when everyone is accepted.

To be able to create a strong community with no judgment, it is important to teach our children empathy and compassion. Learning how to accept others for who they are breaks down the barriers to creating a rich community.

5 Ways to Build Compassion and Empathy in Your Children

Hands up who has been judged for saying the 'wrong' thing, wearing the 'wrong' clothes, driving the 'wrong' car, being the 'wrong' weight, living in the 'wrong' house, eating the 'wrong' food, living the 'wrong' life?

Hands up who has judged someone for wearing the 'wrong' clothes, driving the 'wrong' car, being overweight, being the 'wrong' race, color or age or raising their kids the 'wrong' way?

Here's your challenge – for the next hour, you won't judge anyone. You won't judge your parents, you won't judge your children, you won't judge the person you just walked past on the street.

Imagine a world where people didn't judge each other.

Imagine a world where people showed kindness and compassion to others.

Imagine for a second if parents didn't judge each other, but worked together to raise happy, healthy children. Imagine if there was no judgment in mothers groups or on the playground, but parents actually helped each other out.

What if people in workplaces didn't judge each other, but worked together to get the best outcomes.

Imagine if you didn't judge the homeless person you walked past on the street last night – instead you talked to them with care and compassion.

You have probably all heard the story of when the father got on the subway late at night with his 5 children who were all being loud and misbehaving in one way or another. Catching the disapproving look from the other people in the carriage, the father apologized. 'Sorry, I am on my way home from the hospital and just trying to imagine how I will handle my first night without their mother'.

The world can be a cruel place. It can lack compassion and kindness for people who are judged and for those who judge.

Why do people judge others? Judging others is a natural instinct because they look, sound or behave differently to us. It is a primal instinct to defend territory and we take a fight or flight response and this may have worked for cave men that needed to protect their own areas, however today it runs deeper.

The main reasons for judging others is a lack of understanding, perceived views from experience or upbringing or a lack of empathy and compassion.

Perceived views and lack of empathy and compassion are largely learnt and built on behaviors stemming right from our childhood and upbringing.

As parents, we have a responsibility to teach our children about differences, educate them about others so they have a genuine understanding and build on their empathy and compassion. We can teach our kids how to be non-judgmental.

1. EXPOSE YOUR CHILDREN TO PEOPLE FROM DIFFERENT WALKS OF LIFE

> *'It takes a good deal of character to judge a person by his future instead of his past'* ~ RALPH WALDO EMERSON

I took my children with me some days to the Wayside and people judged me for taking them to a 'dangerous' place with drug addicts, people with mental illnesses and the homeless. The difference was that I knew most of the people who came there and the encounters my children had with these people were always a raw and beautiful experience for my kids and also for me to see how each interacted with people who they would not normally speak to.

One meeting that sticks out in my mind is when my children met Cathy* – an Aboriginal lady in her early 40s with bright pink, curly hair who was homeless at the time. She had a rough side and had experienced life in ways different to many. My son sat with Cathy on the bench and asked her where she slept at night and she described where she slept and what it was like. As a mum of 9, she had a way with kids. They talked about what it was like to be homeless and how different her life was to his.

They talked about what happened when it rains in the middle of the night and where she gets her breakfast without a kitchen. They talked about what bathroom she used and where she put her clothes without a cupboard. She loved my kids as soon as she met them and they got to know each other quite well over the next few months. There was no judgment from either side. Now when it rains at night, my kids wonder where Cathy is and hope she has found somewhere dry to sleep for the night.

If we allow our kids to meet people from different backgrounds, we are building on their empathy, compassion and understanding of differences.

2. ALLOW YOUR CHILDREN TO EXPERIENCE MANY CULTURES

> *'It's not what you look at that matters, it's what you see.'*
> ~ HENRY DAVID THOREAU

If you can, live in a different country. When my kids were little, we lived in the States. My husband was doing a university masters with military members who were serving from all over the world and they brought their families to live in Washington DC for the year. My kids played with children from Pakistan, Holland, Norway, Lebanon and the UAE. They also went to school with American kids and learnt the pledge of allegiance. It was a great immersion into a new culture.

Here are a few other ideas to experience other cultures:

- Go on holidays to places with cultures vastly different from your own
- Meet local families who are from different cultures and invite them for dinner
- Each city generally has an enclave of particular cultures with many great restaurants to visit e.g. China town in Sydney, Brick Lane in London, Washington DC has an Ethiopian quarter
- Go to your local Japanese, Italian, Chinese, Vietnamese, Thai restaurants and meet the chefs
- Put the world map up on the wall in the dining room and pick a different country each week to look at their culture or cook a different meal from a particular country
- Children generally learn a language at school – look at the culture specific to the language or encourage them to learn another language

3. Educate your kids about differences and celebrate differences

From a very young age, children know that people look or speak differently to them.

Take the time to tell your kids it is OK to be different and talk about the differences they have observed. It is not OK to judge that person for being overweight or being a different race.

Talk to your kids about difference religions, cultures, appearances, illnesses and how other people live their lives.

Talk to them about mental illness, about alcoholism, about children with autism and about people's idiosyncrasies. If these things are not foreign to our children, they will accept the differences they observe as normal everyday occurrences and not judge it for being different.

By talking to our children we provide them with a vocabulary to discuss differences.

4. TELL THE TRUTH, NOT OPINION

In a park with a friend and our children, there were four men were sitting on the chairs in turbines with long beards. Her 5 year old son asked 'Are they religious people mom? Are they OK?'

No matter her views or judgment she replied – 'They are from the Sikh community that live close by us. You know Alibi* from your school is from this community'.

She could have shrugged it off and not answered in a truthful way – she could have shrouded it with opinion to illicit fear or pity. Her answer was straight up and her son knew he was in a safe environment with different people around.

No matter your views and opinions, if you can tell the truth around differences, our children will make have the chance to form their own ideas.

5. USE NON-JUDGMENTAL LANGUAGE

Our kids will take our lead from the language we use. If we use judgmental language, our children will. Our children will soon pick up if we are racist, sexist, biased or judging others and copy.

Being mindful of the language we use will give our children the right words to use around others to show kindness and compassion.

A family with a little girl was sitting in the waiting room of a doctor's surgery. A Pakistani man walked in and sat down on the bench next to the little girl. The dad stood up and sat in between the little girl and the man, obviously uncomfortable with his appearance. The doctor came out and called the family in and the Pakistani man followed – it turned out he was the donor of the bone marrow that saved the little girl's life months earlier.

If we educate our children about differences, teach them about other cultures and provide them with opportunities to meet people from many walks of life – we set our children up to be compassionate,

kind adults who can form strong communities without judgment.
(*names have been changed)

CHAPTER 14

Teach children about emotions

Emotional resilience is borne out of knowing how to deal with emotions and react accordingly. Given our first reaction to a crisis or adverse situation is usually emotional, we need to teach our children about emotions and how to use them.

If you have a car crash, your first response might be anger, mixed with regret or fear. Your body goes into fight or flight mode and you can feel the response occurring with your heart beating faster, sweaty palms, hot head, and tingling toes. Ideally then, your rational brain then kicks in and you know what to do next. You are acting out of rational decision making, rather than purely reacting emotionally or irrationally. Our children don't have this emotional development yet and so it is our job as parents to guide them and coach them to recognize and understand the emotional responses they are going through and give them tools and strategies to navigate these emotions. This will allow them to respond well to adversity and setbacks and also mitigate the major lows that life can throw at us.

How do we teach emotions to children?

We help our children recognize the different emotions they are feeling by exploring with them, coaching and role modeling. We then guide our children with tools and strategies to deal with their emotions.

Here are two simple, practical ways to help children recognize their emotions:

FEELINGS LADDER

Together, help your child develop a feelings ladder (Fig. 5). Start by drawing a ladder with rungs and write the emotions from bad at the bottom of the ladder to good at the top of the ladder. Talk about each emotion and when they have experienced it. Then get them to write simple ways they can climb the ladder.

Here are a few examples of when I taught this to a class of 8 year olds. They already had many of their own natural coping mechanisms such as 'giving mummy a cuddle' or 'holding a soft toy'.

The most important part here is to extend their thinking on coping mechanisms and then put it up on their bedroom wall and refer to it when they are angry, frustrated or sad and ask them to reflect on what they can do to climb up the ladder.

RED/GREEN FEELINGS CHART

In a similar way to the Feelings Ladder, this chart (Fig. 6) helps children develop their own strategies to move from the 'bad/difficult/unhelpful' (or Red) feelings to the 'good/positive' (or Green) feelings.

To make your own Red/Green Feelings chart, on a piece of paper draw three columns. The first column is the 'Red feelings column', the second is the 'Strategies and tools' column and the third is the 'Green feelings column'.

Brainstorm with your child all the feelings that make them feel 'bad' or negative and write them in the Red column. Then write down all the 'good' or positive feelings in the Green column (or third column). Now this is the fun part. Together write or draw all the strategies and tools your child has to help them move from the 'Green' feelings to the 'Red' feelings.

TEACH CHILDREN ABOUT EMOTIONS

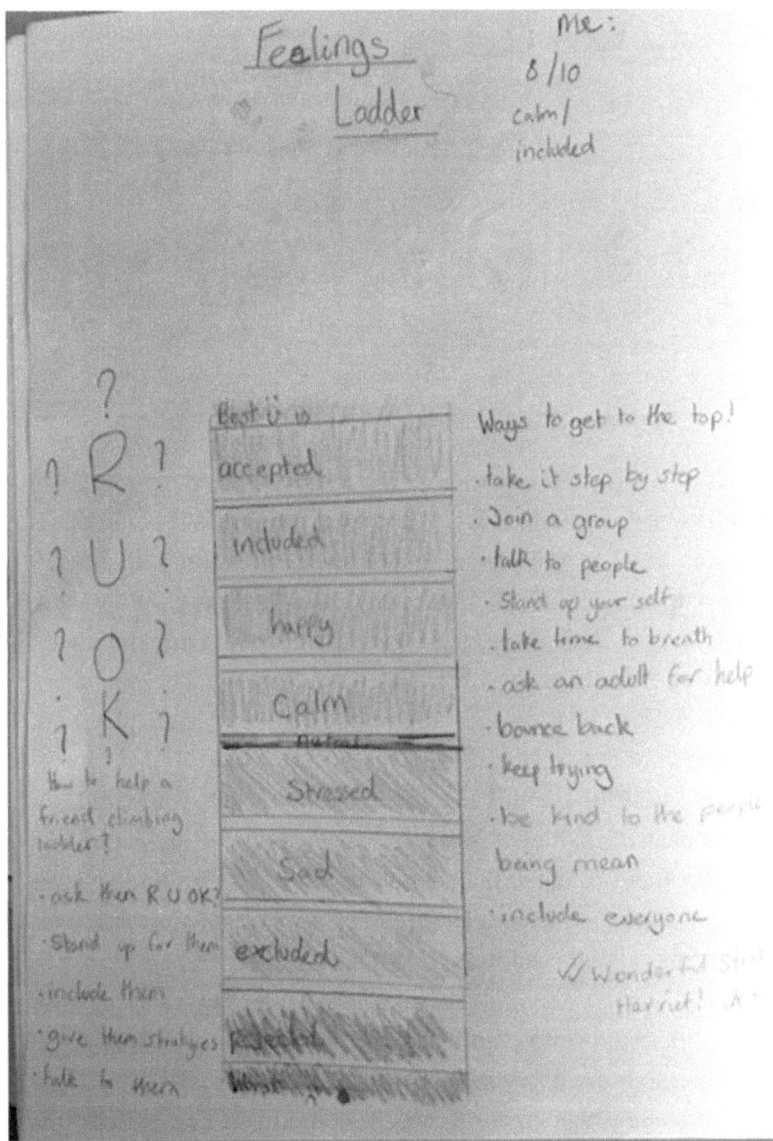

Fig. 5: Example of a Feelings Ladder from an 8-year-old

It might look something like this...

Red feelings	Strategies and Tools	Green feelings
Angry	- Cuddle with mum	Happy
Sad	- Play the guitar	Confident
Upset	- Bounce on the	Excited
Fearful	trampoline	Strong
Tired	- Climb trees	Positive
Bored	- Watch television	Warm
Lonely	- Bake a cake	Loved
Disappointment	- Listen to music	Grateful
Terrible	- Read a book	Calm
Bad	- Play with friends	Free
Cranky	- Build Lego or a	Playful
Confused	block tower	Amazed
Scared	- Go for a run	Surprised
Frustrated	- Go to the park	Relaxed

Fig. 6: Example of a Red/Green Feelings Chart by a 7-year-old

It works best if you do it together and if your child is old enough, they can draw or write the emotions and the strategies. If they are involved, your child will more likely use it as a tool. Allow them come up with their own strategies first and then coach them with others you think might work. Once you have made your chart, display it. Put it on their bedroom wall to refer to or in the playroom so your child can see it and use it.

You could also use this as a way to find out where your child is at emotionally throughout the day. Are you feeling Red or Green? And then get them to name their emotions. For children under three, faces of these emotions or the feelings bears might work better to help them name the emotion. If you have more than one child, you will need to make a feelings chart with each one of them, as they will have different positive and negative feelings and also different strategies to move between the two.

The feelings that are the hardest for our kids to deal with are the big emotions like anger and disappointment. Here are some practical ways to deal with both.

Anger: A big emotion

Activity: Listen to your kids playing together for 10 minutes. Notice the reaction if someone steals a toy from the other, or someone doesn't play fairly in the game. What is their reaction?

More often than not, it is anger.

Anger is one of those huge emotions that adults struggle to deal with and it is even harder for children. One thing to remember is that anger is a normal emotion to go through, especially as a child and especially boys aged about 7 or 8. When you are a child or a parent watching your child lash out when they are angry – it can be hard for everyone involved.

Children share the same emotions as adults but do not know how to control their anger. They need direction and some need it much more than others. Angry outbursts are OK if they are not physically hurting you or any other person – if this happens, it is probably time to seek professional help.

Here are some tips to help your child deal with their anger.

Remain calm. Anger is a big emotion. It is big for us as well as our children and it might take all your energy to do remain calm, but if you can be calm during your child's angry outburst, it is worth it. Once they have 'flipped their lid', there is nothing you can do so it is best to stop talking, make sure there is no danger and ride out the storm. Once they have finished the outburst – it is then time to teach them about emotions. Stay calm, ride out the storm and it will be over more quickly.

Be a role model. Children will be watching us to see how we react when we are angry. If you yell and kick things when you are angry – it is almost guaranteed they will. If they see you loose your cool and not deal with it in a way you want them to, they will copy. If you are angry and you talk through it – tell your kids you are angry because of (whatever it is) and you are going to deal with it by walking around the block – they will know that it is normal to be angry and put their own strategies in place to deal with it.

Know what sets your kids off. Trust your intuition here. You know your own children the best. You know what sets them off and while you can not avoid it every time – try not to put them in a situation where you know they will be angry.

My son is terrible when he goes to bed late. We were away this particular week and he went to bed after 9pm three nights running. By the fourth day, he was tired and cranky and the smallest things set him off. I knew he was tired so on the fourth night, I put him to bed at 7.30pm – there was some resistance as we were staying at his cousins place and they were all still up. But I knew him and I knew his limits of being tired and acted accordingly.

It is important for you to respond to the needs of your child in this situation and know what their triggers are. Another trigger for us is the last day of the school holidays. We have spent enough time together and everyone is ready to get back to their routine – and so there are often angry outbursts. I know they will happen and I am prepared for what will ensue.

Do a needs check. When your kids are already angry and you don't know the reason – do a needs check. Are they hungry, feeling unsafe, overwhelmed, tired, hot or thirsty? Sometimes a child's first default to not having their needs met is anger. They often don't even know why they are angry so check if they need something.

Validate your child's feelings. Anger is a big emotion and children are often scared by it. They react without thinking and during or after an angry outburst they can feel embarrassed and upset. You need to reassure them that being angry is OK and turn it into a lesson.

Be consistent. If your child is having angry outbursts, you need to be consistent and start as you mean to go on. So, if your child is having an angry outburst and you can stop it with a cuddle – do it. If they don't want to be touched, maybe you need to walk away or speak to them in a calm voice. If you loose your cool once, then cuddle them the next time, then yell the next time, then walk away the next time – you can see how this will give the wrong message. As their parent, discover the best way to reassure your child and then be consistent with it.

Teach your kids how to 'get over' feeling angry. When being angry is your child's default to deal with setbacks or adversity, it can often help to give them practical solutions to resolve their anger. The Angry Wheel of Choice (Fig. 7), created by Jane Nelson from the Positive Discipline Association when created together will help your child see it is OK to be angry and find their own strategies to bounce back.

Together you will create a spinning wheel and they will come up with practical solutions, like play with the blocks, listen to music, jump on the trampoline, cuddle with mum, draw pictures and fill in each piece of the wheel. When they are angry, you can refer to their Anger Wheel of Choice to choose one of their 'go to' happy activities to help them get over their anger.

Children are often angry when they get in the car from school. The safety of the car and seeing you is enough to tip them over the

1) Teach your children that feelings are always okay, but what they do is not always okay.

2) During a time when your child is feeling calm, show him or her the Anger Wheel of Choice and go over the respectful alternatives for expressing anger.

3) When your child is angry, validate feelings and then offer a choice, "What would help you now—some positive time-out or the wheel of choice?"

Fig. 7: Anger Wheel of Choice. Source: Jane Nelson, Positive Discipline Association, Atlanta USA

edge. Add this to not finishing their lunch or being hungry at the end of the day and it can be a pressure cooker for disaster so be prepared for the onslaught and pack food, remain calm and put on some good music. They feel it is OK for them to do this because you are their safe haven.

DISAPPOINTMENT: ANOTHER BIG EMOTION

Disappointment is another one of those big feelings that can override any rational thinking. Children need to feel disappointment to be able to develop their own methods of coping with it.

A few months ago, my son came home from school and told me with a heavy heart that he had not been chosen for the school cricket team.

For the past month, unknown to us, he had dreamed of playing for the school team and thought about what he would do on his first match. How he would wear his cricket pads, hold the bat, run after he had smashed the ball for a 6 and he had practiced and practiced in our yard. At the tryouts, he dropped a catch and that was the end of his quest. To hear he wasn't going to be in the team was a huge disappointment for him. I felt helpless for him and wanted to fix it, but to fix his disappointment would have been counter productive for both of us.

Right at this moment, I needed to 'be' with him.

I needed to validate it 'sucked big time' he didn't get into the team. I didn't need to offer him treats to make it better or take him out for dinner to ease the pain or tell him there is always next time. I needed to let him feel what disappointed was.

By sitting with him and hearing how bad it was, I was letting him experience the feeling of disappointment and could show him it was OK to feel this way. I talked to him about my own disappointments and we could share together. While we were talking, he was building his own strategies and tools to bounce back from the disappointment in his head – building these strategies is a life long skill we can teach out children.

Teaching our kids how to bounce back from disappointment, sadness and negative life events – rather than 'fix it' for them – is one of the most valuable gifts we can give as a parent. Building resilience and strength to climb from the low moments to higher moments is invaluable.

4 WAYS YOU CAN HELP YOUR CHILD THROUGH DISAPPOINTMENT

1. Allow your child to feel the disappointment. Don't rush in to comfort straight away or offer a food treat to make it 'better' – let your child feel the disappointment for a time. You want your child to be able to create its own solutions for bouncing back. Of course if they are crying inconsolably, you would give them a cuddle or soft touch on their back, but otherwise it is not a bad thing for our child to feel the disappointment.

2. Validate your child's feelings. Agree with your child that it feels bad not to be accepted into the cricket team or to not be chosen in the choir. Don't use words such as 'you just weren't good enough this year, maybe next year'; they don't need to associate negative emotions with it. Offer words of encouragement and validation.

A little girl was crying next to me at the kids swimming carnival. I asked her what was wrong and she told me how she was in the marshalling area ready to try out for butterfly and got scared – now she was watching the race she was meant to be in and was disappointed with herself for not going in it. As she talked more and her friends gathered around, she decided it was not such a bad thing after all and managed to convince herself she did the right thing with a lot of validation from all of us. She actually didn't know how to do butterfly and wanted to keep her energy for the freestyle finals that were coming up.

3. Brainstorm solutions to bounce back. Talk to your child about strategies they used to overcome their disappointment – it might be at the dinner table that night when you are reflecting on the day. Don't dwell on it or single it out as a significant event, but talk about some of the strategies they used when they are no longer emotional over the event and can think more rationally. You could combine it with other lessons they might have learnt from that day or get other members of the family to reflect on their own strategies for bouncing back from disappointment.

4. Children live in the moment. As adults, sometimes it feels like disappointment can last for hours or even days. But for children who very much live in the moment, it lasts as long as the next cute puppy walks past. So don't dwell on it with them or over catastrophize the situation.

Feel it, validate it, and talk about some strategies to bounce back from the disappointment and then move on. They will be ready to move on pretty quickly and you need to as well. By the time my husband came home the night my son didn't get into the cricket team, I was still disappointed for him and he was over it. He had moved on to the next thing to strive for. While not dwelling on it, do reflect back on it at some stage to ensure lessons have been learnt for the next disappointment.

Other big emotions are fear, sadness and loneliness. If your child is feeling any of these, you can apply the same practical solutions to help them bounce back. Please seek professional advice if is the lows are getting too low and you have used all the strategies you know to deal with them.

Teach your child to fail

Our children make mistakes and fail every day – and so do we. It is the way we have shaped our children to deal with these mistakes and failures that are crucial to bouncing back from them and dealing the outcome. It is also the quickest route to success.

It is OK to fail. Our children need this message loud and clear. All too often, I see children in the classroom cover up their mistakes, rub them out until there is a whole page of flaky, white pieces of rubber or worse, lie about their mistakes. When I start the beginning of the year with a new class, I invent the 'Rubber bus'. I walk around the room with a jar and everyone has to put their eraser (or rubber) on the bus and they will see them at the end of the year. Children need to make mistakes to learn to learn and it is amazing at the end of the year to look back through their books and see how the writing, ideas and content has improved.

Because we are in such a rush for our children to succeed, we have lost the big picture idea that it is OK to fail. As a result, our children feel bad about making mistakes. And we have risen the bar so high in the achieving stakes and competition, that when they do fail, they don't know how to cope with it.

To teach our children to fail, first we must allow them to take risks.

This starts right in our playgrounds. Playgrounds have changed significantly since we were kids. The height of the monkey bars has been lowered, the slippery dips are also lower and less steep with a protective edge and see-saws are non-existent. This is because they have been deemed too risky. A child 'might' get whacked by a see-saw, fall off when they are coming down a steep slippery dip or fall from the monkey bars. We then put soft fall underneath incase they do fall to soften the blow.

When we were living in America, a family who lived a few doors up had three children. They were each a year younger than my kids and would often find their way into our backyard. They loved the climbing frame in our yard and the swings, but most of all they loved our trampoline. After a few weeks of them coming over, their lawyer mother came in and saw them playing on the trampoline. She very plainly asked me if we had indemnity insurance for our trampoline and that was the end of her children coming into our yard. Of course we didn't and we weren't about to get it. Sadly, because I didn't want the risk of her children getting hurt on our trampoline, they no longer came into our yard.

We have become a risk adverse society and this is sadly impacting on our children to take age appropriate risks and fail. A good double bounce on the trampoline soon teaches you to jump at the same time as the other person or move far away. If you bang heads from jumping, it will hurt for a while and then you will get back on and go right on jumping. Every mistake you make on a trampoline teaches you a lesson to bounce back and improve your technique for next time.

Do your kids climb trees? If you answered yes, you are among the minority.

Only 1 in 3 children climb trees today. Our kids don't climb trees because it is too risky. When climbing a tree, children need to use judgment, risk assessment, skill, focus, planning and dexterity. They need to navigate which is the best branch to stand on and grip on to get up. They need to navigate through branches and they need to strive. They need to strive to get to the top. And when they reach the top, they need to cautiously navigate getting down again. Will they take the same path as on the way up? Will they forge a new path? How will they get past the spiky branch? Will this branch hold them? If it is a successful tree climb, confidence levels are high. If it is unsuccessful, they will try again and again until they succeed. This increases their persistence and ability to strive.

- How about lighting a fire with your child?
- Or lighting a match and watching it burn?
- Or doing experiments with boiling water?
- Or riding a motorbike?
- Or climbing onto a boat or paddleboard?

- Or swim in the ocean?
- Or surfing?

For each of these activities, there is some risk involved. However, if we set up the rules and expectations around each one and talk about the safety concerns with our kids, it helps them to learn how to fail and make mistakes and then solve the problem.

On a family holiday, my husband taught my kids to surf. It was brilliant to watch my 10, 9 and 6 year old catching waves and actually standing up to surf. They were excited they had mastered a new skill but with it came lots of time under the surfboard, getting dumped in the waves and using persistence and striving to keep going. Over the week, each of them had their moments of giving up. With encouragement and healthy competition to do it like the other kids, they kept on going. It was a teachable moment and life lesson in striving, persisting and failing until you succeed.

By teaching our kids to take a risk and fail we are helping them grow and develop their own strategies for bouncing back and what it feels like to succeed. We are teaching them to innovate and explore possibilities. Some of the best risk takers are entrepreneurs who has learnt to fail and rebuild. Richard Branson was one of them.

We all know it doesn't feel good to fail. It is human nature to want to sweep the feeling of failure under the carpet, however the real learning happens when our kids sit with the failure or mistake and feel it. Don't be too quick to jump in and fix it for them, rather be with them to feel it and strategize. When they have learnt how to bounce back on their own from these setbacks, they are more likely to continue to use this pattern over and over – making a mistake, learning from it, doing it better next time.

Sometimes when our children are strategizing about failing, it is easy to blame someone or something else rather than to take the blame themselves. My 10 year old is quick to blame others, rather than feel the pain and it is a constant lesson we are teaching her to allow her to take the responsibility of failure or mistakes she makes herself. We are all very good at talking ourselves into a situation and if you can believe it was someone else who messed up and not you, your confidence remains intact and you can easily carry on – without ever feeling what it is like to actually make a mistake, learn from it and do better next time. There are no problem solving skills involved and no learning. This is when bad habits form around failure.

When our children are taking risks, they need to be age appropriate. A 2 year old obviously won't be able to climb the tallest tree in the yard, however by the age of 5 or 6, they might. Each child is different in the risk they will take and they will need to be nurtured to experience the risk, failure and bounce back scenario.

EMOTIONAL INTELLIGENCE: TEACH IT EARLY

Another way to help our children build resilience is to teach them emotional intelligence.

You have probably heard the term "emotional intelligence" many times, but what exactly is it? And why is it important for children to develop their emotional intelligence?

Emotional intelligence, or emotional quotient (EQ) is a "person's ability to identify, evaluate, control and express emotions." It helps us communicate with others, negotiate situations and develop clear thought patterns.

Leading psychologist and author, Daniel Goleman argued in his *New York Times* bestselling book, *Emotional Intelligence: Why it can matter more than IQ* (1996), that EQ is a more important measure of how successful a person is, than Intelligent Quotient (IQ). Goleman's revolutionary ideas around the science behind EQ started the movement towards incorporating EQ into many organizations and school curriculums.

IQ measures a person's academic intelligence, whereas EQ measures emotional intelligence – a person's ability to interact with others or 'social intelligence'. People with high IQ do not always have social intelligence and may lack the skills to be successful in many current work environments.

According to a Forbes article in 2013, "research carried out by the Carnegie Institute of Technology highlights 85 percent of financial success is due to skills in 'human engineering' including your personality, ability to communicate, negotiate and lead.' And only 15 percent is due to 'technical knowledge." People with a strong EQ make good leaders and managers and are better at working collaboratively in team environments.

If we foster EQ with our children when they are young, we are setting them up to communicate well, develop strong relationships, negotiate tricky situations, be leaders in their field and according to TalentSmart even earn more money. They will be more empathetic and compassionate to their friends, partners and own children, relate more easily to others and have a greater self-awareness.

Can we teach our children emotional intelligence?

Absolutely. Some kids are more instinctively in tune with their EQ and will be ready to deal with new or different situations and people more easily. Others have a lower EQ from the start and need us to teach them in a more focused way. Regardless, all children need to have their EQ nurtured and be supported through the minefield of emotional experiences as they grow.

Since its inception, the education system has strongly focused on developing IQ and improving children's intellectual ability. However, since the advent of the EQ movement started by Daniel Goleman in 1996, many schools are now teaching children to identify their own emotions and perceive the emotions of others around them. However, there is still along ways to go in many educational settings and so parents need to play a pivotal role in fostering their children's EQ.

FOUR WAYS TO BUILD EMOTIONAL INTELLIGENCE WITH YOUR CHILD

1. Help your child recognize their own emotions. Once you help your children "name" their own emotions, whether it be frustration or anger or disappointment, they can start taking ownership. Here you will not only spell out what they are feeling, but in what context it is affecting others. When they are feeling upset or discouraged, ask them to describe what they are feeling or get them to write it down or draw it. Do it often so they get to know what it feels like to be sad or angry or frustrated and they will learn to name their own emotion. Don't forget to do it with good emotions too. My daughter's preschool teacher uses images of emotional teddy bears and the children pick which bear they are feeling. They say what made them feel that way and explain the emotion. For example, my daughter picked the happy bear because she felt happy after playing on the swing with her friends.

2. Talk about your own emotions with your child. The best way to foster emotional intelligence is to show it. Tell your children how you are feeling and allow them to perceive it for themselves. We often only think about emotions when they are big and hard to deal with, like feeling disappointed or sad or angry and your children will likely know when you are feeling any of these. You can also demonstrate here how you deal with your own big emotions and "get over" anger or disappointment. It is important to talk about the positive emotions too. For example, I am feeling so happy today because we just bought a house. Tell them what it feels like for you. And demonstrate how your emotions might affect theirs. As a parent, our own emotions have been sparked or triggered by something our child may have done (good or bad). One of the most important things here to remember is not to blame your child for making you angry or sad – they haven't made you angry – you have made you angry. This is invaluable to teach our children, however it is a hard concept for adults to understand and even harder for children. Once they know their own trigger points with you and others, it will be much easier to control their emotions.

3. Recognize the mood or feeling inside your house. The mood and feelings change within your house. If you have people over, it might feel fun and jubilant. If you wake up on a Sunday morning and the house is quiet, it might feel calm and relaxed. Discuss these differences with your children. Allow them to recognize the different moods inside your house and see how their own emotions impact what happens in the house. At some stage, especially in the holidays, the mood feels so high it might explode and this is the time you would take your children to the park or break the pattern somehow – discuss this with your children.

4. Recognize the mood or feeling when you go places. Going into a crowded shopping mall will "feel" different from being at a playground. Talk to your children about the different moods. A sunny, hot day will feel different to a rainy, cold day and it will be different for each person. As we approach summer, I was asking my own children which season they like best. Two said summer and one said winter so we explored why we liked each better and it came down to memories and activities, but mostly moods. Two liked being outdoors with space to run around and a less crowded, relaxed atmosphere. One liked winter and to be in the house playing games with us because it was happy and fun. Each could explain the feelings or emotions that went with the seasons. Try this activity with new and familiar places you go and at different times. So if you go to the supermarket and it is really busy, ask them what mood they pick up and then if you go the next time and it is really quiet, they will pick up another mood.

Bringing awareness to the emotions and moods that are felt or perceived in different situations helps your child assess the emotional intelligence of each place. If they have just started at a new school, they will know what the mood is or if something changes for the day at school, they will be able to deal with it much more easily after knowing what they feel and how it affects them. They will also be aware of how they pick up the moods of others in their day.

Building emotional intelligence now will help your child be a good manager, good leader, be able to contribute to a team environment personally and professionally and more importantly have the ability to develop strong, connected relationships now and later in life.

Stress – Another big emotion

By teaching our kids how to form relationships, building a solid relationship with them ourselves and giving them emotional stability by teaching them about emotions and how to react to them, we have set them up to be emotionally strong.

However, we want our children to use the right tools to be able to deal with the stress everyday life throws at them. Right now teenagers in our society are stressed. The number of young people aged between 15 to 16 years with depression has doubled between 1980s and 2000s. Self-harming is at an all time high and sadly, suicide in this age group has increased. And it's not just our teenagers who are stressed. I have seen this first hand teaching in public schools where children as young as 6 are anxious or depressed.

Why are our kids so stressed?

In a recent ABC 4Corners documentary, Our Kids, teenagers told why they were so stressed and what they use to ease the stress.

The reasons for stress in teenagers are:

- Increased expectation to do well at school with a rise in standardized testing
- Pressure from parents to perform well at school
- Exams and school pressure to perform
- Peer pressure to be perfect – exemplified by social media
- Cyber bullying
- Increase in marriage breakups with 50 % of all marriages now ending in divorce affecting children's academics, relationships and networks
- Other possible reasons for stress in this age group are:
- Decreased support networks because of a shrinking of community
- No down time because of the hurry up culture we live in
- Unbalanced leisure activities with too much screen time, not enough exercise, not enough sleep, too many structured activities and little enjoyment
- Referred stress from parents who are stressed from leading a fast paced life

We need to teach our kids coping mechanisms to deal with stress now so they can incorporate it into their lives.

Here are some ways our kids can deal with their stress in the short term:

- Exercise – exercising released the 'happy chemicals' our body needs to alleviate stress. This could be in the form of organized sport, yoga or other physical activity like kicking the football around the park with mates or going for a run.
- Relaxation – listening to music or doing a formal relaxation will again promote 'happy chemicals' to alleviate stress.
- Recognizing stress – being able to recognize stress is important to be able to act on it. Talk to your children about the possible signs including headaches, feeling irritated, feeling overwhelmed and not on top of things or having a sick feeling in your stomach.

- Meditation – a regular practice of meditation can also alleviate stress. The app Smiling Minds is great for younger kids and Headspace for older kids.
- Practicing gratitude – keeping a gratitude journal allows you to focus on the positives of life and look for them each day
- Having a positive outlook on life – knowing and finding the positives, rather than the negatives helps alleviate stress
- Talking it out with a parent, teacher or adult – if you need to talk, find someone to talk to
- Positive inner critic – if you help your child develop their positive inner critic, they have self confidence, self belief and a strong dose of courage to get through their worries
- Getting enough sleep – getting 9 to 11 hours of sleep a night will reduce stress levels and increase awareness and clarity
- Eating good food – alleviating stress by eating well, not eating junk food, can help.
- Knowing when to get professional help – stress can sometimes go too far and the mechanisms aren't working so know when to reach out for this professional help, either at school or in the community
- Having fun! – Life can get too serious and this is when stress creeps in, go out and have some fun with your family or friends.

PART 3

Nurturing a healthy body
(Physical resilience)

WHAT IS PHYSICAL RESILIENCE?

The third element of raising a resilient child is nurturing a healthy body or building a strong, healthy child who is able to bounce back from illness and other body trauma, well.

What we put into our children and the habits, behaviours and routines we develop around eating, sleeping, exercise and good hygiene now will ideally carry them through their lives.

We want our children to be able to maintain their stamina and strength and recover quickly from an illness and return to a healthy state of wellbeing. We want to instill the positive nutrition, sleep habits and ways to stay healthy to prevent disease and illness. And we want to raise active, engaged children who can enjoy physical activity now and as a life long habit.

There are many ideas and conflicting advice given on the best way to stay healthy; however, if you look at our bodies their basic needs are food, water, air and sleep – other contributors to a healthy body are exercise, good hygiene and a balance between each factor.

The building blocks for a healthy and strong body start right from the moment our baby is conceived, or even before. This is why a healthy pregnancy and giving our baby the best chance to develop in the womb is so important. To maintain a healthy body for our children, they need sound sleep, good nutrition, plenty of exercise and good hygiene as well as creating good habits around each of these.

CHAPTER 15

Start with a healthy pregnancy

From the moment of conception, the molecular and genetic makeup of our baby is underway. We help it to grow arms and legs, heart and lungs, a face and even little eyelashes. Whatever we put into our own body when we are pregnant is directly crossing the placenta and nourishing and growing our baby. It is still a miracle we are able to conceive a baby and grow it within our womb and along with that comes a responsibility to provide the baby with the best environment to grow and develop.

Here are ways to maintain a strong, healthy pregnancy.

Nourish yourself and your baby

When you are pregnant it is important to nourish your body the best way you can, because everything you are putting in your body is transferring directly to your baby.

The Australian Dietary Guidelines prescribes to pregnant women eating a balance of the five food groups including proteins, carbohydrates, dairy, fruit and vegetables and drinking plenty of water. Protein helps a baby grow and develop, iron is crucial for brain development, foliate is essential for healthy neural tube development and zinc helps build bones and teeth. Aside from maybe the foliate, if you have a healthy diet and if you listen to your body you will be getting all the essential nutrients for your baby to help it grow and develop.

The best way to stay healthy is to be in tune with your body to guide you with what you and your baby need. The early cravings may be a sign you need more of the nutrient that is in that particular food or drink and similar with the aversions.

When I was pregnant I had terrible morning sickness for the first 19 weeks with all three children and during that time I couldn't tolerate the smell or taste of steak or any other red meat. I ate chicken and found other ways to get the required amount of iron I needed to grow my babies. With my middle child, I have to confess I had a major craving for chocolate cake and had a piece most days of my pregnancy, which might explain why he was born 4kgs. I am pretty sure there were no required nutrients in cake, but perhaps my body needed the sugar hit and calories to sustain him.

What's all the fuss about alcohol and drugs during pregnancy?
Drinking alcohol and taking drugs during pregnancy can have detrimental effects on the baby's brain and development. When the substance crosses the placenta and enters the developing baby's bloodstream, it can end up with a higher blood alcohol level than you. This relates to the size of the baby in relation to the size of you. With overuse of alcohol and drugs, it affects brain development and can result in low birth weight, which can slow language and speech development, attention span, learning and behaviour. A large amount of alcohol results in fetal alcohol syndrome, which will impact the child for the rest of their lives.

Research and educate yourself on pregnancy and birth to make informed choices
Talk to friends, family or people who you trust who have been through a healthy pregnancy, read books (like Robin Baker's Baby Love) or find information from trusted sources on the Internet. If you have a concern, consult your doctor or midwife for advice. There

is so much information available, but you need to find the advice and information that you resonate with the most and adapt and modify it to work for your lifestyle and body. Learn about how the baby grows and how your body changes. Research different ways to give birth and find the one you feel most comfortable with.

Move your body
Keeping up your exercise regime or finding an activity like swimming or yoga can help facilitate and nurture your changing body. While it's not healthy to be obsessed with how much weight you put on during pregnancy, it is something to be mindful of and doing something each day will ensure your body maintains a healthy weight range and you will bounce back after you give birth.

Get enough rest
In equal measures of exercise, your body needs rest to grow a baby. In the first and third trimester when your baby is growing exponentially, your body has a natural mechanism to get you to rest. You often feel so tired; you can't function – so rest. Take the time to grow your baby and put your feet up. There are not many other times in your life when you have the perfect excuse for an afternoon nanna nap!

Enjoy your pregnancy
While you might not enjoy every minute of your pregnancy, take time to reflect on the miracle that is happening inside your body right now and know how clever you and your partner are to create another living human being. Imagine what their face and hands will look like and what the moment will be like when you meet your little bundle. Take the time to notice and enjoy the changing shape of your body. Nine months is a short time in a lifetime and a time to celebrate.

Take care of your emotional health

With hormones soaring high and impending changes to your body and your lifestyle on the horizon, it is important to nurture your emotional health. When I was again lying in the bottom of the shower with severe morning sickness in the 14th week of my third pregnancy, I needed to use all my strength and optimism to get through it, with two toddlers already running around. It is important to connect with others during this time, seek help and support and ensure you are mentally and physically strong to deal with the challenges and changes. It is also important to take some time out for yourself. Soon enough you will have a little baby to care for and put all your focus into. If you already have children and this is a second or third pregnancy, you will need to make sure you have time for yourself to keep your emotions in check.

CHAPTER 16

Encourage sound sleeping habits

Getting a good night's sleep for our children is just as important as adequate nutrition and exercise to help them be physically resilient.

Many physical and chemical changes happen in the body during sleep, especially when we fall into the deep sleep stage, that is crucial to brain development, growth, digestion and healthy development. As a parent it is important to provide the right environment for kids to get all the sleep they need.

So why do kids actually need sleep?

Here are 8 reasons why your kids need to get a good rest each night – some may surprise you.

1. SLEEP HELPS KIDS GROW. The growth hormone (GH) responsible for making our kids bones grow is mostly released when our kids sleep with the most intense period of release shortly after the start of the deep sleep phase. Growth is a complex process that requires several proteins to stimulate events in the blood, organs, muscles and bones. This could explain why babies sleep at least 50 per cent of their time, to help them grow in a crucial stage of development. The old saying of 'you could almost watch a baby grow in its sleep' rings true here.

2. SLEEP HELPS KIDS MAINTAIN A HEALTHY BODY WEIGHT. Sleep deprivation can lead to children becoming overweight for the following reasons:

Firstly, sleep deprivation affects the creation of the hormone leptin, which signals us to stop eating and so when we haven't had the right amount of sleep; we keep on eating without a signal to stop. When this happens in kids on a continual basis, they overeat which increases the chances of an unhealthy weight range.

Secondly, when parents are coached to recognize their babies cues for hunger as opposed to other distress signals and begin to soothe without feeding – such as swaddling or cuddling – babies will sleep better and are less likely to be overweight.

Thirdly, when children and adults alike are tired, they crave higher fat and higher carb foods and tend to be more sedentary, increasing the likelihood of obesity.

3. SLEEP FIGHTS OFF INFECTION. When we sleep we produce proteins known as cytokines, which the body relies on to fight infection, illness and stress. In other words, by sleeping, we are helping our body bounce back from any illness it might be fighting. As a double effect, an increase in these proteins makes us sleepy, which then explains why we are tired if we have a cold or flu. It is our body's natural way of getting us to sleep. With little sleep, there are less cytokines available to ward off infection.

4. SLEEP KEEPS OUR HEARTS HEALTHY. Kids who have sleep disorders have excessive brain arousal, which can trigger the fight or flight response many times a night. If the levels of glucose and the stress hormone, cortisol remains high at night, there is more likelihood of diabetes, obesity and heart disease. It could also increase the likelihood of mental health issues including anxiety and depression.

5. SLEEP REDUCES INJURIES. When you have had a good night's sleep, your coordination is in balance and information processing and reaction times are high. However, for kids who have less sleep, studies show they are more likely to have injuries that require medical attention. The reason for this is because, when we are sleep deprived, our metabolic rate decreases and glucose metabolism drops by 30-40 per cent, affecting our energy production.

6. SLEEP INCREASES ATTENTION SPAN. This will come as no surprise that if your child gets more sleep; they have a more sustained focus and attention span. Research shows that children who sleep fewer that 10 hours a night before the age of three are three times more likely to develop hyperactivity and impulsivity by the age of 6. Dr Owens, M.D, director of Sleep Medicine at Children's National Medical Center in Washington DC says that 'For school-age kids, research has shown that adding as little as 27 minutes of extra sleep per night makes it easier for them to manage their moods and impulses so they can focus on schoolwork'.

On the flip side, children with ADHD are more vulnerable to the effects of too little sleep. Children with ADHD are three times more likely to have a hard time falling asleep or staying asleep each night.

7. SLEEP HELPS KIDS CONTROL THEIR EMOTIONS. Sleep deprivation affects kid's moods. Kids who have had enough sleep are able to control their emotional impulses better when they are faced with a stress, adversity or setbacks. It is difficult to focus and pay attention and you are more irritable when you are sleep deprived resulting in anger and frustration over smaller issues. Sleep deprivation affects the serotonin levels in our bodies where low levels can lead to depression or a significant change in mood.

8. SLEEP BOOSTS LEARNING. Sleeping boosts memory and learning for all ages of children. A research study on newborns showed that while they sleep they are actually learning. Investigators played certain sounds for sleeping newborns and then puffed gently on their eyelids over a period of time. Within 20 minutes, the sleeping babies had already learned to expect the puff of air at the end of the sound – visible by their squinting eyes.

Another study of preschoolers showed that the daytime naps were important for memory development. A researcher taught preschoolers a game similar to memory. The first week, they all slept on average 77 minutes during the day. The following week, they played the same game and didn't sleep. When they didn't sleep, they forgot on average 15 per cent of what they had learnt as opposed to when they did sleep. The kids scored better on the game when they woke up and the day after too.

Sleep increases the connections of the neural pathways to aid in learning and memory. The learning we do in the day reactivates in the brain in the deep sleep period resulting in specific dendric spine growth – which helps us retain information and process memory.

Something to think about in the school holidays.
A study by the Dalhousie University in Nova Scotia found that if our children get as little as one hour less a night over a period of four nights, the effects of sleep deprivation are visible. Think about this on your next holiday when bedtimes may be lax or you let your children stay up when you have friends to stay for a long weekend or you let them stay up to watch a sporting event such as the Olympics or World Cup. It's fascinating how quickly it can have an impact.

Is your child getting enough sleep?

NEWBORNS AND BABIES (0-12 months) For the first few months, babies will need 16 to 18 hours of sleep over a 24-hour period. They usually don't sleep for longer than 3-4 hours at a time. By 3 months, babies need 15 hours of total sleep spread across the day with 3 naps per day and by 6 months; it is 14 hours and generally two naps per day. By 12 months, a baby still needs 14 hours of sleep a day to help with the huge growth and development in this time.

TODDLERS (1-3 years) Toddlers need 11-14 hours of sleep over a 24-hour period. This could be a 2-3 hour daytime sleep and 8-12 hours at night. The daytime sleep is as important as sleeping at night to consolidate the learning that happened in the day and to give your very active toddler a rest.

PRESCHOOLERS (3-5 years) Preschoolers need 11-13 hours of sleep each night.

When children are transitioning out of the daytime sleep, this can be a hard time for children and their parents. It is harder for some kids than others and once they do drop their daytime nap, they will reset into a good nighttime routine again. This can be a transition period from 2-3 weeks to 3-4 months or even longer in some cases. When kids are dropping their sleep, the days they do sleep generally mean they will go to sleep much later at night – parents need to be flexible at this time and understand it is a temporary period. Unfortunately there is no magic bullet to 'fix' or ease the pain of dropping the sleep, rather remember it is a transition period and their sleep will realign again shortly.

SCHOOL AGED KIDS (5-12 years) School aged children need 9-11 hours of sleep every night. They are active at school and learning something new each day. This downtime helps them consolidate their learning and refresh them for the next day.

TEENAGERS (13-18 years) Teenagers still need 9-10 hours of sleep a night, however their pattern will change as they develop. Teenagers need less sleep at night between 8am and 10pm and then they make up for it in the morning by needing to sleep in.

Here are some signs your child may be overtired:
- Overly irritable or grizzly
- Angry and frustrated for no particular reason
- Clumsy or falling over a lot
- Craving carbohydrates or sugary foods
- Falling asleep in the car
- Unable to focus and concentrate on instructions
- Lethargic and sedentary, flopping around

SLEEP ISSUES: BABIES 0 TO 12 MONTHS

When I work with families with babies and toddlers, some of the biggest struggles are around sleep. If both the kids and the parents are well rested, it is much easier to get through the many challenges that face us each day and life is more enjoyable. Besides, children are healthier, more focused and there are often less behavioural challenges.

With newborns and babies, the challenges are generally how to get a baby to 'self-sooth', where should the baby sleep and how much sleep is enough. There is also the major issue of sleep deprivation for the parents and practical ways to deal with lack of sleep and caring for a baby. These answers are different for every family and every baby, however setting good habits and routines early around sleep help a child develop healthy sleeping patterns right from the get go.

DOES CONTROLLED CRYING WORK?

The controlled crying method of getting babies to 'sleep through the night' is popular among the parenting fraternity. The idea espoused by many, well-meaning professionals, including Robin Barker is that if you leave a healthy, well fed, changed baby to cry for varying amounts of time, they will learn to go to sleep. When I tried controlled crying, it broke my heart. It felt unnatural to leave a little baby on its own to cry and according to leading pediatrician at Sydney's

Prince of Wales Private Hospital and Royal Hospital for Women, Dr Harry Chilton, it is unnatural.

Dr Harry believes that controlled crying is a good sales tool to help stressed out parents, but doesn't do any good for the baby. Here are the reasons why controlled crying doesn't work:

Firstly, human babies are born the most premature of any other animal species. This is so their large heads can contract to fit through our narrow pelvises. Because of this, babies need 'high intensity, contact based care for a long time'.

Secondly, the primary source of baby nourishment is breast milk in the early days, which is very low in protein, so it's quickly digested and needs replacing frequently. It takes about 35 minutes for a baby to digest breast milk, which is part of the reason babies are waking up frequently unsettled and need a feed.

Thirdly, until the age of about 8 months a baby has no sense of object permanence. You know when they start to drop things from their highchair tray and watch it fall to the ground and think it is a great joke when you pick it up and they drop it again. This is when they have grasped the concept of knowing an object leaves and comes back or can be seen again. So if a parent leaves, they have gone forever in the minds of our little babies and so of course they will panic.

Fourthly, before the age of 6 months, children have no learning centres in their brain yet and so cannot learn to sleep one night and remember it the next night.

The fifth reason is little known and has the most impact on our baby. Loss of parental contact is a serious danger signal for young babies and they are designed to cry and cry until it is restored. Beyond a certain point even a hysterical baby will stop crying, often quite suddenly which Dr Chilton calls extinguishment. An unprotected, crying baby is telling it predators where it is and instinct tells it the parents have vanished, 'and that saber tooth tiger that killed them is also close' so it goes silent to survive.

These facts fall in line with the positive parenting idea that children cry because of an unmet need. A baby is no different. It is crying because it needs something and our job as parents is to work out what it is that child needs. This is not easy on the 189th night of having 2-3 hours of sleep a night in a row and neither is it rational to think at 3am of sensible, practical ways to calm a screaming baby. However, if we apply love at this time of the morning and nurture the needs of our baby, we can set them up to be emotionally stable children.

Right from this age, we are building a relationship with our child and building their attachment mechanisms. If our whole ideal is to connect with our kids and nurture and protect their emotional development, it doesn't work to leave a baby crying on its on for long periods again and again.

CAN A BABY SELF-SOOTH?

The short answer is no. For the same reasons it can't be expected to sleep longer than three to four hours, our babies are dependent upon us for their survival, including self-soothing. Babies sucking reflex is strong and providing opportunities for them to suck, including a breast, pacifier or cuddly toy may help. Some kids have a natural tendency to suck their fingers or thumbs to sooth themselves – however the best way to sooth is touch. A hand on their back as they try to sleep or a reassuring cuddle.

With my own children, it didn't work to cuddle them to sleep because when I put them down into their cot, as soon as their head touched the mattress, they would wake straight back up. It was easier to lay them in their cot or bassinet when they were still happy and they would generally drift off to sleep. However, when my youngest was about 3 months old, every time I put her in her cot to sleep during the day she screamed. So we put her in the pram and walked three times a day (with a 4 and 2 year old) so she would sleep. This only lasted a short time, maybe 3 to 4 weeks and then the cot was her preferred place again.

Every baby is different and will go through many different cycles. The best way to help a baby sleep is do what works for you and your family. Know the cues of being tired – as opposed to hungry or needing a nappy change and then remember that this period of time they are babies is only short in the scheme of life. Some days will just work and you and your baby will sleep well. You will try to remember every little step you took to replicate that the next day, however the next day it won't work at all. It is mostly trial and error to see what works best for you and your baby.

Sleep routines

As a newborn, the sleep patterns can be all over the place but by about 4-6 weeks, you can get your baby into a routine that will work for you.

This simple routine generally works with the families I work with who have babies 0 to 6 months. It is Feed/Eat – Play – Sleep – Repeat.

It looks like this:

Feed/Eat – start the routine with a breast or bottle feed or if your baby is 6 months (or older), with food.

Play – once the feed is over, allow your baby some time to play. This is a lovely time to interact with your baby and really start building that solid, loving relationship. For newborns, the play will be much shorter and may just involve talking with your baby, singing a little song, bathing it or having a cuddle until they are tired again. From about 6 weeks, you can add in tummy time and more interaction. At 4 months, lying under a play mat for 15 minutes might be part of the play routine or going for a walk in the sun. It can also work for a 6-month-old baby who will be having 3 sleeps a day. The play will be more engaged and for a longer period. By 6 months, babies will probably be rolling, if not starting to crawl and so the play might be rolling around a big mat with some toys to stimulate.

SLEEP – When you see the tired signs in your baby (getting grizzly, yawning), its time to put your baby to sleep. This can be a sleep in a cot, crib, baby pouch or out walking with your baby in the pram, depending on their age.

REPEAT – this routine starts every time you breast or bottle-feed your baby. When your baby wakes up, start again. Feed, play, sleep and repeat.

I like this routine because there is no definite time frame around it. The times will vary depending on what you need to fit into your day, what time your baby wakes in the morning and how many feeds your baby is having. For example, a newborn that is feeding every two or three hours, it will be a short cycle. For a baby who is 6 months old and having three sleeps a day and between four feeds, the cycle will be longer. It is adaptable and flexible enough to fit in with most babies and lifestyles. Obviously, the feeds at night won't involve a play period, however they do allow time to change a nappy in a dim light and have a lovely little talk or cuddle. While the nights are tiring, the extra snuggles are priceless. Some of the best memories of my son as a baby are at this time of day when it was just he and I, no other distractions or other children vying for attention. His smiles on the change table and little cooing noises were beautiful.

SLEEP DEPRIVATION – HOW DO YOU HANDLE IT?

Sleep deprivation is a form of torture and if you have had a newborn, you know what I mean. It is amazing how we exist on such little sleep in the early days, however with some inspiration, a community and self-care, anything is possible.

When my third child was 2 or 3 weeks old and I had taken my

eldest to preschool – the day ahead looked long with a newborn daughter and a 2-year-old son. I had had about three hours total sleep that night and cumulated since my daughter was born, it was pretty minimal. A lovely mother at the preschool asked me to come next door for a cup of tea and told me 'some days are dogs and some days diamonds – run with the dogs and marvel at the diamonds'. I have kept that in my mind ever since and it sure helped through those early days when the days just seem so long and I was constantly juggling washing, feeds, sleeps and life with a newborn and toddlers.

People used to also tell me at this stage that the days are long, but the years are short and I didn't believe them until my children all went off to school. I couldn't imagine where those years of having babies had gone. They were now all in their school uniforms and off to have their own adventures. The long days of physically carrying them in and out of the car, the prams and daytime sleeps were all behind me. The nappies, feeds and baby cries were finished. While these days are hard, they are precious and we will again get a full night of sleep.

The dangers of sleep deprivation with a newborn is that our rational decision making is impaired and we start to make decisions based on emotions and feelings, rather than sense. It can also alter our moods substantially and coupled with our already enhanced hormonal state, can lead to much sadness and stress, and at the extreme, postnatal depression.

Here are some practical ways to get through those early days:

- Ensure you have a support network around you. You don't have to do this part of having a baby all by yourself so make sure you have people around who can ease the load and share in the joy and exhaustion. Good friends, family, a community centre, a mothers group, old friends, mothers at school/preschool are all good places to start. When my friend had twins and already had

a 4 and 2 year old, making an extra dinner for them all, picking up bread and milk on the way over or dropping around for a cup of tea were all imperative to her sanity. Connecting with others and sharing your day, outside the needs of your baby, are important.
- Take time for self care. Whatever your favourite indulgence is – do it. If it's a haircut, massage, pedicure, walk, cup of tea with a friend or shopping make some time for it. If you have someone to leave your baby with that is great. If not, take it with you. Make time for you, even with your baby in tow. Getting out is a great way to bring some normalcy back to having a new baby.
- Find inspiration and hope. By having a positive outlook on your situation, it is much easier to get through the day. Look for inspiration from quotes, from other mothers who have done it or are doing it with you or from online and real life groups. Or maybe keep a gratitude journal to look for the positives.
- Find your groove. You need to find your own groove to enjoy this time of being a new mum or having a newborn and know that it takes time to adjust to any change.

Sleep issues: 2- 7 years

Dropping the day time sleep

Between the age of 2 to 3, children drop their daytime sleep. This can be challenging for both the child and the parents. Every child is different in when they drop their sleep and how long the transition takes. It can be anywhere from one week to 6 months.

Because it is a transition period, there is no quick fix to dropping the sleep, rather an adjustment period. During this time, your child may fall asleep in the car on the way home from preschool and then not go to bed until 10pm (despite serious attempts). Or if they don't have their sleep, they can be overly irritable and overtired at dinnertime and then crash out early. Remember, it is a normal transition and once they do drop their sleep, a normal sleep routine and pattern will resume.

How do you put your kids to bed and keep them there?
As children get older, the sleep issues changes. With children from the age of 2 years to 7 years old, the challenge with sleep is generally getting the kids to bed at night and keeping them there. By setting up good boundaries, routines and habits around sleep, children can learn how to put themselves to sleep, go to bed when they are asked and stay asleep throughout the night in a respectful, loving way.

Imagine this….

It's 7.30pm. You have had a long day. You have spent the day juggling kids, housework, and work and you have finally made it to the kid's bedtime.

You are looking forward to making a nice hot cup of tea and putting your feet up (after folding some washing and cleaning up the kitchen of course).

The last thing you feel like doing is going through another bedtime power struggle. You need some time to yourself or maybe it would be nice to spend a few hours with your partner.

You kiss your little one good night and head out of the room and feel that sense of relief – your mind already on the next thing you need to do WITHOUT KIDS under your feet.

Two minutes later you hear the pitter-patter of footsteps coming towards you – *'I need a drink'*. Fine. That only takes a couple of minutes to make and then your child will be back to bed.

Five minutes later… pitter-patter of tiny feet again coming at you. *'I need another cuddle'*. Fine that also will only take a couple of minutes too and then back to bed.

Ten minutes later… *'I can't sleep'*. All you want to do is have some quiet time. Now you are getting annoyed. Right. Breathe. Put child back to bed.

Child is in bed crying. They are actually crying so loudly you think the neighbours will come in or worse they will wake the other sleeping kids in your house. So you tell your child in the nicest possible way to GO TO SLEEP.

It is now 8.15pm. 45 minutes since you first put your child into bed and you and your child are both over this situation. You are thinking you will never get that conversation with your husband – your child is overtired and now will take even longer to go to bed. Do you give in and lie with your child until they go to sleep?

Do you leave your child to cry the house down? Or do you put them back to bed time and time again until you are both exhausted?

This is not the first time this power struggle has happened this week. In fact, it happens most nights. And some nights you might lie with them, some nights you might try this technique and other nights they just fall blissfully asleep.

There is a practical way around this same scene that happens every night. Here are some ways to put your kids to bed and keep them there in a loving, respectful way.

1. SET THE BOUNDARIES.

You are the parent. You set the rules. Kids LOVE rules when they are achievable and well founded. When kids are at school or day care, they follow the rules. They know the physical boundaries of the school and stay within them. They know the expectations in the classroom, and they genuinely try hard to stick to them.

You need to set up the boundaries around bedtime and be CONSISTENT.

If your child knows they can come out of their room to tell you they are thirsty and you get them a drink, then tomorrow night expect them to do the same.

If they can't sleep and are allowed to come out of their room to tell you they can't sleep, expect that tomorrow night it will be OK too for them to pitter-patter to you after lights out.

If neither of these sounds OK – you set the rules that work for you and communicate it with them.

You set up the expectation that, when you have read a book, given your child a cuddle and kissed or sung a bedtime song together and then turned out the light, that signals it is time to sleep.

Once you have set up these boundaries, it then becomes the expectation and then habit.

The same boundaries here won't apply for every family and you will need to determine the rules *you* want to set up with your children. As your kids grow or your circumstances change (you move house, you add a new baby, you go away on holidays) the rules may need to change to suit the situation.

If you give them a drink before bed, they cannot possibly be thirsty five minutes later and so this is not an excuse for coming out of the room. If this is a constant reason they come out, put a water bottle next to their bed.

Set the rules around coming out of the room once you have put them to bed – the rules might be they can only come out if they need to go to the toilet or have a cuddle if they are scared.

The other important rule is to set the time you will put your kids to bed. Is it 7.30pm bedtime, lights out at 8pm. Is it 7.30pm bedtime full stop? Set up the routine in the lead up to bedtime.

What are your rules right now? Think of the four rules (or boundaries) that are important around your kid's bedtime right now. Are there any new rules you need to add for a smoother bedtime?

Tonight, when you put your kids to bed, communicate the old and new rules and boundaries with them and start right away. It might take a couple of days to embed the new routine, but once they know you are serious and these are the expectations, it will work and they will only come out of their beds when they absolutely need to.

2. SET UP THE ROUTINE.

The lead up to bedtime is important and you need to set up the routine well so everyone knows what it is.

Work backwards.

If the rules you have just written above say that your kids are going to be in bed by 7.30pm, then have dinner at 6pm.

Between dinner and bed, make this quiet time or this might be when your kids need to run around to get out the last burst of energy for the day or is might be bath time.

What about when they get home from school? Is it at 3.30pm and do they do homework straight away? Or if they are younger, is this playtime? Or do they come home at 5pm when you collect them from daycare or after school care?

Whichever the scenario – having a set routine that your kids know will help them settle before bedtime. It is important that you and your kids know the routine so you can both follow it.

Here are some things to think of to set up your routine:

- When will your child have a bath?
- After the bath, where will the child's pajamas be? Should they hang their towel up?
- Do you have to stay in the bathroom with your small children or are they old enough to have a shower on their own while you cook dinner?
- When will your child do their homework?
- What time will you have dinner? Where will you have dinner? Will you have dinner together as a family?
- Is television (or electronics) part of the schedule? If so, how much?
- Is exercise part of the schedule? If so, when?
- Will you clean up the kitchen straight after dinner or when the kids are in bed? Is it your job or your partner's job or do you

share cleaning the kitchen? What will the kids do when you are cleaning the kitchen?
- Do you have a set meal plan each week or do you have food ready to go if the night routine turns to custard?
- What time will your child go to bed?
- When you put your child to bed, will they read a book or will you read to them before they go to sleep? Where will you read to them – in the playroom or in their bed?
- Or will lights go out straight away?
- Will you sing a song together to signal lights out or say a prayer?
- Do they have a night-light? And if so, who turns it on and off?
- When do they do their teeth, go to the toilet and have a drink?
- If your child gets up after your routine, what is your plan?

Here is what a typical nighttime routine might look like for a toddler.

5pm Pack away everything from the day including playroom and bedroom

5.15pm Bath time

6pm Dinnertime (at the dinner table with family)

6.45pm Clean teeth, go to the toilet and get ready for bed

7.15pm Story time and a cuddle with a parent (either in bed or on the couch)

7.30pm Get into bed, lights out

Here is what a typical afternoon and nighttime routine might look like for a school aged child.

3pm Finish school

3.30pm Afternoon tea

3.45pm Start Homework (it is much easier to complete homework as soon as children get home from school when they are fresh and still in learning mode. Trying to do it at 7pm after dinner is too late for kids to focus and concentrate on learning).

4.30pm Free time for playing, relaxing, talking, helping to prepare dinner, inventing, creating, being kids

5.30pm Bath/shower

6.30pm Dinner (at the table with family)

7.15pm Pack away toys, homework, pack school bags for the next day

7.30pm Clean teeth, go to the toilet

7.35pm Get into bed and do independent reading or read to a parent or older sibling

8pm Lights out

You may be surprised in both routines to see no technology. Technology within two hours of kids going to bed interferes with their sleep patterns. Especially the rapid fire television shows or video games stimulate a child's brain to the point it takes at least 90 minutes for it to be ready for sleep.

A visual that helps to set up the night for younger children is a checklist or bedtime routine planner (Fig. 8). While you are establishing the routine, your children can work through the checklist, which you both create together, each night until it becomes habit.

It might look something like this:

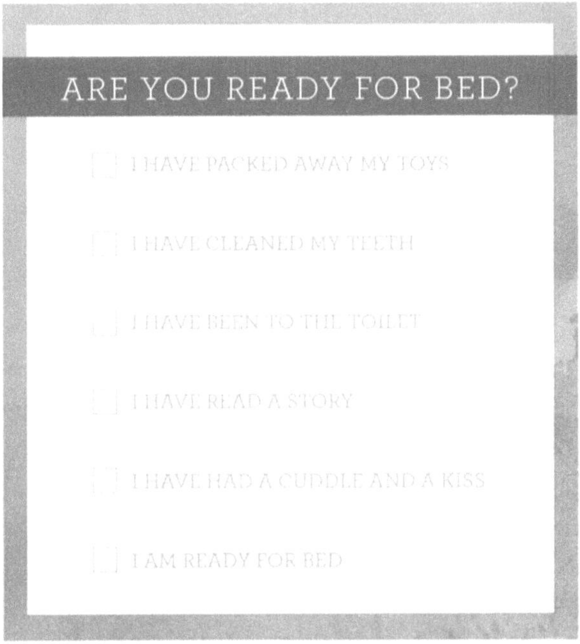

> **ARE YOU READY FOR BED?**
>
> ☐ I HAVE PACKED AWAY MY TOYS
>
> ☐ I HAVE CLEANED MY TEETH
>
> ☐ I HAVE BEEN TO THE TOILET
>
> ☐ I HAVE READ A STORY
>
> ☐ I HAVE HAD A CUDDLE AND A KISS
>
> ☐ I AM READY FOR BED

Fig. 8: An example of a checklist to put on the bedroom wall for a 3-4 year old

3. BE CONSISTENT

Now you have your rules and routines in place, the absolute trick is to be consistent. You have set up the rules and routine with your kids, now you need to stick to them.

Don't waiver until you all know the deal. Your partner will need to be a part of it too and the kids will need to follow the rules and routine.

So, when your child comes down for a drink, you now know if you get them one or not. And if not, don't get them a drink after you have put them to bed again!

If your child can't sleep and you say it is OK for them to get into your bed and go to sleep – you will need to say yes to that request every night so be prepared. If however, you want your child to stay in bed, say no and put them back to bed. Not Super Nanny style where you can't look at your child and over and over again, as that creates more power struggles, but with a reassuring cuddle and kiss with a reminder of the rules to not come out.

Putting your kids back to bed 100 times a night is fraught with escalating the situation around sleep and creating a whole new avenue for power struggles. Going right back to building a relationship with our child, we need to help them feel safe and secure around going to sleep and ensure they have that sense of significance and belonging they crave at this age. Also, if this is the case, there is often something else going on for this child that is preventing them from wanting to go to bed and sleep.

4. MY KIDS ARE STILL NOT GOING TO SLEEP

Children being able to get to sleep easily and stay asleep is heavily linked to good nutrition, getting enough exercise, limiting technology before bed, mental state, not being too over stimulated from extra curricular activities or other activities and believe it or not, getting enough sleep – if your child is overtired, it will take longer for them to fall asleep.

If your child can't sleep, ask yourself these questions:

- What has my child eaten today? Was there too much sugar, not enough protein or not enough food with nutritional value?
- Has my child had a lot on at school lately – mentally or physically?
- Is there a stress I don't know about affecting their mood?
- Has my child been physically active today?
- Is my child unwell or getting unwell?
- Has my child had enough sleep this week?
- Are we trying to pack too much into the week or day?

- Did my child watch or play with technology up to 2 hours before bed?
- Has the schedule or routine changed?

All of these factors make it difficult for our child to fall asleep and this will need to be factored into the boundaries and routines you have set up.

5. Be realistic

Life with kids is chaotic and changes regularly. A routine is important, but you also have to be flexible enough for it to change and, when it does change, be prepared for your child to challenge you on your consistency. This is often when most of the trouble happens – once we are inconsistent in times of change, it is much harder to get back to the routine and boundaries that we have set up in the first place.

It takes time to implement a new routine and rules and it also takes time for your child to be OK with your consistency. Depending on what is going on in life around your kids, this checklist won't work every night – so be prepared to have some nights where it will take longer to put your child to sleep than usual, depending on life's unforeseen challenges and changes. Remember that child's bodies are designed to sleep. They will fall asleep eventually and your job is to provide the best environment and set them up with healthy habits, routines and expectations around sleep so they can do it on their own.

Parents can come unstuck when they try to control children's sleep with bribes, rewards and punishments, rather than proving the tools and strategies to help them sleep. Getting your kids to sleep can quickly become a power struggle and when it does, children rev up, become overwhelmed and it takes longer to sleep. If your children are healthy and have had enough exercise, adequate nutrition and know the bedtime routine, there should be no reason to have struggles at bedtime.

MY CHILD IS SCARED OF THE DARK

Between the ages of three and five years of age, children's imagination goes into overdrive and it is difficult for them to separate reality from fantasy. This often results in disturbed sleep, nightmares and fear of sleeping because of what they might 'see' at night.

CASE STUDY: 5 YEAR OLD JULIA

Julia is a 5-year-old girl who lived in a two-story house with a long hallway. She was scared of the dark and recently had decided there was a ghost in the hallway leading to her bedroom that wore a 'long black coat, something over its head and all you could see was its eyes'.

Perceived or real, in the mind of a five year old whose imagination is in overdrive, it can be a scary ordeal. The 'ghost' was stopping her from going to sleep and waking her up at night in her nightmares.

Julia's father did a few practical things to allay her fears. The first thing he did was validated and respected her fears, rather than brushing them off. They were real to Julia and her dad was taking the time to listen to her concerns without shaming or punishing.

Julia's dad then helped her make a 'magic potion that gets rid of ghosts at night'. Together, Julia and her dad filled up a spray bottle with water that had been infused with every prickly weed, piece of grass, 'not pretty flower', nuts, berries and bark from the garden that she could put beside her bed and spray when she felt scared. The spray bottle empowered her with a tool and some reassurance she would be OK at night. They also developed a nightly routine of saying 'shoo shoo' as they walked down the hallway to ward of the ghost. After a few weeks, the ghost was long gone, she was easily going to bed and the nightmares had stopped.

Here are some further ideas to help kids with their scary bedtime thoughts or dreams;

- Put a fish tank in your child's room and impress upon them that monsters or robbers are scared of fish
- Put a plant in their room and tell them the elves and fairies who live in it will protect them
- Retell a personal story of being scared of the dark yourself when you were young
- Make an anti-baddie device
- Take a mental photograph, draw it, rip it up and put it in the bin to get rid of the bad thoughts
- Put Fireman Sam or a superhero figure near a window to stop the monsters and robbers getting in
- Put a salt light in your child's room so there is some natural, calming light

Some more long-term, underlying thoughts on children being scared of the dark are:

- Find out if there is anything going on with your child that they may be scared of and could be manifesting at bedtime as an 'I'm scared'
- Monitor sugar and food toxin intake that coincide with bed time struggles
- Spend an extra 10 minutes cuddling, reassuring and settling before bed
- Don't let your child watch the news before bed
- Limit screen time of all sorts after dinner to calm their brains before bed
- Do a relaxation exercise before bed: Take five deep breaths with your child and have them exhale saying, 'I have nothing to be afraid of' five to 10 times depending on how unsettled they are or use the app Smiling Minds to get a child friendly meditation

- Is their routine about to change or has it changed recently?
- Think about the book you read before your child goes to bed and make sure it isn't scary

Another researched idea to help with being scared of the dark is visualization. During a quiet time in the day, get your child to recreate what the scene looks like when the lights go out with their own toys to have a more visual picture of it and then discuss how you can change the picture with them. When you put your child to bed that night, remind them of the scene and how they can physically or mentally change it.

It is important to know that fear of the dark should only last a couple of weeks at a time. If it lasts longer, or is a reoccurring theme it is best to get some additional help from your doctor or medical professional to see there is no underlying concern.

BEDWETTING

Bedwetting is a common reason for children waking at night, with 40 per cent of all three year olds wetting their bed most nights. There are many and varied causes for bedwetting and besides having to get up in the middle of the night to change the sheets, it's the way we react as parents that has the greatest impact on our kids

If we react to it with shame or frustration, our kids will feel it. Children don't wet the bed because they are lazy, it is generally developmental or there is a family history of it. If you were bed wetter, chances are, your kids will be too.

Here are some ideas to deal with bedwetting:

- React well. Remain calm. Reassure your child. Change the sheets and go back to bed. Don't over catastrophise. And what ever you do, don't shame your child for wetting the bed. It can quickly become a psychological issue of shame and affects self-esteem now and when your child is older.

- No one else needs to know – especially siblings who will tease or poke fun so keep it between you and your child.
- Limit fluids before bed.
- Put a waterproof mattress protector on your child's bed.
- Make sure your child empties their bladder before they go to bed and when they wake up to get in a good habit of bladder health.
- Toilet train well. Some advice from my first child's preschool teacher was when you take a nappy off for good; don't put another one on – not even at night. This makes perfect sense because when you put a pull up on at night, you are sending a mixed message that it is OK to do a wee at night in bed, but not during the day. While it may be necessary for some children, it is much harder to get out of the habits of using pull ups after your child is toilet trained so do it all at the same time. A few nights of wet beds when your child is 2 is easier than to wean children off pull-ups at 6.
- If you wet the bed as a child, talk to your child about it so they know they are not alone.
- Normalize it. Tell your child that kids sometimes do wet the bed and it is not something to be worried about. It will stop and you will clean it up right now so your child can get back to sleep.
- Kids might wet the bed because of a sudden change or emotional upset. They might have just started preschool, moved house or parents divorced – once the upheaval has settled, the bed wetting will too.

By the age of 6, children have generally stopped wetting the bed. If you are worried at any stage along the way, consult your doctor.

SLEEP WALKING

Sleepwalking is common with 30 per cent of three to seven years having walked in their sleep. It can be disturbing when your child is walking around with their eyes open in the middle of the night muttering unintelligible statements. By the time they are teenagers, children generally grow out of it. The main issue is safety. If you have a sleepwalker, make sure the doors are locked and their environment is safe. It is recommended not to wake a sleepwalker but guide them back to bed as it may cause fear and confusion.

Sleep issues: 7 – 12 years

By the age of 7, children are generally pretty good at going to bed, putting themselves to sleep and waking up in the morning. It is important by this age to have developed healthy sleeping habits to facilitate all the wonderful things sleep does for our bodies when it happens for the required length of time each night. If your child is still not sleeping through the night and you have good routines, boundaries and expectations in place and you are worried, consult your doctor.

As parents, it is important to be consistent with the routines and expectations around sleep and provide the best environment for your children to get their much-needed sleep without controlling, punishing and bribing.

CHAPTER 17

Maintain good nutrition

Good nutrition is one of the major building blocks for ensuring our children build and maintain a resilient body and are able to bounce back from illness or adversity.

Nutrition is the intake of food and 'good' nutrition is the intake of an adequate, well-balanced diet in relation to the body's dietary needs. Poor nutrition then can lead to reduced immunity, increased susceptibility to disease, impaired physical and mental development and reduced productivity. In children, nutrition affects energy levels, stamina, focus, emotional state, growth, development, long-term physical health, capacity to fight illness or disease and can also impact a child's behaviour. With a balanced diet, our children can thrive, rather than just survive.

In the first two years of a children's life, optimal nutrition is key to healthy growth and cognitive development and sets the building blocks for a healthy body weight for the rest of the child's life.

The World Health Organsiation recommends that:

- Infants should be breastfed exclusively during the first 6 months of life.
- Infants should be breastfed continuously until 2 years of age and beyond.
- From 6 months of age, breast milk should be complemented with a

variety of adequate, safe and nutrient dense complementary foods. Salt and sugars should not be added to complementary foods.

There is a lot of conflicting advice about good nutrition when it comes to kids and at every turn there is a website, billboard, Facebook post, another parent help book or television advertisement telling parents the best way to feed their children.

Largely, a parent's commonsense needs to prevail with nutrition and the knowledge that what we feed our kids will impact on our child's ability to think, grow, develop and respond to adversity. It is important to have an understanding about what we are putting into our children's bodies and how these choices will help or hinder their growth and development in long-term.

It is our job as parents to provide a well-balanced diet and just as importantly, to help our children develop a healthy relationship with food. The healthy relationship comes when we expose our children to many food choices, not punish and control their every meal, allow them to be part of the preparations, make choices around food and instill good habits about when and what to eat. Food, just like love and sleep are basic necessities and too often they are used for punishing or controlling a child rather than for nourishing and as part of the healthy fabric of the family traditions.

Realistically, it is not OK to feed our kids hot chips and hamburgers for every meal because of the high fat content and basic lack of nutrition. However, hot chips and hamburgers are OK to have every now and again or as 'sometimes' foods. Conversely, putting a child on an extreme diet that rules out any of the major food groups is not be a healthy way to provide adequate nutrition either.

Children have a natural propensity to be active. They want to run, jump, swim, ride and move quickly. Imagine a 6 year old if they had Fruit Loops or Cocoa Pops for breakfast, had a donut and chips for recess, chicken nuggets, hot chips and a lemonade for lunch, a couple of lollies and biscuits for afternoon tea and then had a cheese burger meal from McDonalds for dinner. This was the same food pattern yesterday and the day before, in fact it has been for most of their toddler years. How are their energy levels? They are probably still running around from all the sugar and preservatives. However, what is their behaviour like? How about their emotional stability? If they come across an obstacle, can they overcome it or do they fall apart at the smallest challenge? Are they calm and relaxed when playing or hyped up and overactive? What happens when you tell them it is time to go home?

Imagine this same 6 year old who had had a banana for breakfast, apple for recess, vegetable soup for lunch, an orange for afternoon tea and stir-fried vegetables for dinner. This was also their pattern yesterday and the day before and for the last week. How is their energy at the park? Can they actively sustain their focus, stamina and play for a long period? How is their mood? Are they saying they are hungry all the time? What happens when the parent asks them to go home?

In each example of the 6 year old in the park, there are major food groups missing. The chicken nugget/sugar fuelled child is missing vital nutrients from fresh fruit and vegetables. It is also has a diet high in 'sometimes' foods with no dairy. The fruit and vegetable child is missing carbohydrates and protein, vital for energy sustenance and growth and development. They are also lacking grains and dairy.

How about this 6 year old. Whole wheat cereal with milk, blueberries, strawberries and raspberries for breakfast OR bacon and eggs on wholegrain bread, a fruit boost mid morning, lunch of a chicken, cheese and salad wrap or ham and salad bread roll plus a yoghurt for lunch, egg and vegetable frittatas for afternoon tea and steak and salad for dinner. How will they go with their energy levels? What about their focus, concentration and stamina? And their moods?

When I was teaching a class of 6 year olds, I had a student in my class who was really struggling at school. She was on a Level 4 reader instead of a Level 11. She was struggling to learn her sight words each week and was not progressing. She could answer all the hard questions in Maths when I sat with her one-on-one, but struggled with her concentration on her own long enough to complete an activity on her own or with a small group. She lacked concentration in general, couldn't sit still for longer than five minutes at her table or on the mat with out disturbing others or getting up and walking around the room.

I watched her on the playground and she was active. She would run and jump and play with others for the whole recess and lunch. However, her behaviour was erratic and if her friends didn't do what she wanted, there were meltdowns. She was good at sport.

I started to monitor her eating habits. In fruit break, she would have sugary fruit strips because she didn't like to eat fruit. For recess, she ate popcorn or chips. For lunch, she had a lunch order from school and one day had 15 chicken nuggets. She had Gatorade in her drink bottle instead of water. And for breakfast each morning, she ate Cocoa Pops or Fruit Loops. She was the youngest of five children and spent a lot of time in the car going from one activity to the next eating whatever her mum had bought in a packet.

I met with her parents and I established because she was the youngest and only girl of the family, her parents gave her whatever she wanted to eat. She got to choose at the supermarket and had eaten like this since she was a toddler. She didn't eat fruit, vegetables or diary (except the cheese sprinkled on pizza and hotdogs). She ate mostly fillers in her lunch box with lots of bread and plain pasta. The only meat she ate was ham on pizzas, chicken in chicken nuggets and hotdogs. She was short in stature and small for her age.

After further consultation with the parents and her family doctor, it was established this diet was all too much for her body. She was not getting the active nutrients and requirements needed for healthy body and brain development and this was affecting her learning in the classroom.

When this food pattern has been established from a young age, there is no easy fix. It is a tricky balance because convincing the parents they need to take the responsibility to change their practices is difficult. The parents are also in a habit of eating this way and it is obviously working for their lifestyle.

Unfortunately for the time I was teaching this child, there was no happy ending to this story, as the parents couldn't find a way to adapt their own eating habits to support their child. Perhaps over time, they will find the support they need as a family from a naturopath, dietician or other external partner to help them realign their eating habits in order to provide the right nutrition for this child to help with her concentration and behaviour.

To provide the essential nutrition for our children, the default for advice has got to be based on the well researched and trusted World Health Organisation healthy eating guidelines that have been adapted for each country. In the US, it is the 2015-2020 Dietary Guidelines for Americans. In the UK, it is the eatwell plate from the Department of Health revised in 2007. And in Australia, the Australian Guide to Healthy Eating guidelines.

Similarly in the US and the UK, the main food groups in the Australia Guide to Healthy Eating include:

- **Dairy** – with high sources of calcium, dairy is important for strong, healthy bones.
- **Fruit** – fruit provides vitamins, mineral, fibre and many valuable nutrients that are vital to growth and development and overall health and wellbeing.
- **Grain (cereal) food** – this is the main source of carbohydrates and starch essential as an energy source.
- **Meat, poultry, fish, eggs, tofu, nuts and seeds** – this is the main source of protein for healthy growth and development.

- **Vegetables, legumes and beans** – like fruits, vegetables provide essential vitamins, minerals and fibre vital for growth and development.

Also included on the guide are 'use small amounts and sometimes foods' that includes oils, fats, and foods high in sugar and preservatives including soft drinks, sugary treats, cream, hot chips, hamburgers, juice and alcohol. And drink plenty of water.

These are to be used as a GUIDE. If you were to follow it every day methodically and get caught up in the exact amounts it suggests, eating and cooking would become tedious and more like a diet than cooking and eating to nourish.

Our job as parents is to ensure our children have a healthy relationship with food. By exposing our children to food from the main food groups, we are nourishing their bodies and developing their tastes and their love of food. Eating is one of the fundamental survival needs for our body – without it we die. In many cultures food is celebrated and interwoven as part of the culture. Our job then is to create the healthy habits early on for our children to love food and enjoy the ritual and fun around eating well as well as nurturing a physically resilient body.

What happens when we don't feed our children well?

According to a World Health Organisation, people are consuming more foods high in energy, fats, free sugars, salt than 30 years ago and many don't eat enough fruit, vegetables and dietary fibres such as whole grains. This 'new' diet is wreaking havoc in many areas of our children's growth and development and is affecting their ability to bounce back physically when struck with illness and disease.

The number one concern around children and their current levels of nutrition is childhood obesity. Childhood obesity has reached epidemic proportions worldwide, with United States leading the trend. Currently, 17 per cent of children are classified as obese in the US with 1 in 3 children overweight. In less than 30 years, obesity has doubled in 2-5 year olds and more than trebled in 6-19 year olds. However, this is not isolated to the US.

In Australia, 1 in 4 children are overweight or obese, 31 per cent in Canada and the average across OECD countries is 23 per cent of boys and 21 per cent of girls are obese or overweight. It is estimated that 42 million infants and young children are overweight or obese worldwide and with the current trend 70 million young children will be overweight or obese by 2025. It is the most common disorder of childhood in the developed world.

Under nutrition is also a concern with children now eating 'filler foods'. These are foods that are making children feel full but are lacking the essential nutrients for healthy development of the brain and body. Critical in the first two years, nutrition, along with sleep and physical activity set the building blocks for cognitive development and healthy body weight for the rest of a child's life.

Why is childhood obesity such a problem?

- Obese children are at higher risk of developing diabetes, cardiovascular diseases including strokes, heart attacks and coronary heart disease, asthma, arthritis, some cancers and depression
- 70 per cent of children who are overweight or obese with be overweight or obese as adults
- Life expectancy decreases from between 5-20 years for a child who is obese or overweight
- Obesity leads to low self-esteem and body image which can result in depression, anxiety and loss of confidence
- There is a significant economic cost for the individual and the economy in terms of direct health spending and lost time at school learning
- Poorer ability to bounce back from an illness or disease

When I was living in the US in 2010-2011, I studied a graduate degree in International Health and one of my projects was to research the factors contributing to childhood obesity in the USA and why it has changed so much in 30 years.

This is what I found out:

It won't surprise you that the main reasons there is a childhood obesity epidemic right now because of a decrease in physical activity and an increase in caloric intake. There have also significant changes in food choices, lifestyle choices and the food industry to support these changes.

1. Shift in eating habits. Families are eating out more than ever before. There was a 40 per cent increase in people eating out or getting take away food in the US between 1987 and 2000.

Why do more people eat out? Two reasons:

The first being a change in workforce with more women going out to work. This increased the family's disposable income and decreased the time women spent in the home. In our Grandmother's generation, woman stayed at home and cooked meals, did the washing, looked after the children and kept house. Now, with almost 60 per cent of women working, there are obviously no longer mothers spending the day at home cooking meals. However, families still need to be fed and so convenience became a factor with food intake.

Secondly, at the same time as the shift in workforce, there was a boom in the number of commercial food outlets. Demand was met with supply and the convenience of getting take out on the way home escalated.

Why is eating out all the time bad?
Because food prepared away from home is higher in fat and sodium and lower in calcium and vitamins – the foods children need to maintain a healthy body weight and grow and develop. The food portions also tend to be larger and so there is a higher calorie intake.

2. Decrease in physical activity. Physical activity has decreased across society. Children are less active and so are families as a whole.

There are three main reasons for this decrease:

- Introduction of technology – leisure time for families changed from active, outdoor activities to passive, indoor activities revolving around technology. Families tend to watch more television, use the computer, eat out or watch sport together on television.

- Decreased levels of physical activity at school – schools reduced the requirement for physical activity with only 6 states in the

USA now making PE mandatory. Only 22 per cent of children are meeting the basic levels of activity, 60 minutes of moderate to vigorous intensity physical activity per day and 25 per are classified as completely sedentary.

- Increase use of the car – as a matter of convenience in the 'hurry up' culture we have created, rather than walk to school or to after school activities, kids are driven. It is also because of the perceived or real increased safety concerns in the community and children walking the streets on their own. Sadly, the infrastructure in our cities has also changed and the built environments are not necessarily conducive to children walking.

3. Major changes in the food industry. Since the 1970's there has been a significant change in the food industry including:

- Changes in basis of sugars used in foods;
- An increase in commercial food outlets including fast food chains;
- A propensity for super sizing meals; and
- More targeted advertising to children.

With the introduction of high fructose corn syrup and palm oil, replacing refined sugars in the 1970s and as a result of the change in food demand and supply, manufactures were able to produce cheaper fast foods, prepared meals, snacks and soft drinks. This made it cheaper and more convenient to buy, than preparing meals at home. These already prepared meals were lower in nutrient content and higher in calories, fats and sugars. This became the norm for many families on a daily basis.

Right when people increased the need to eat out, there was a significant increase in franchised food chains including McDonald's and Pizza Hut. The main reason people were repeat offenders at these stores was reliability of product, convenience and value for money. They were also accessible. In 1975, McDonald's increased the convenience factor by adding 'drive-through' – it was now convenient AND fast. The use of drive through changed the shape of the eating habits in the US substantially and now you can 'drive-through' for almost anything you like, including Starbucks and even banks and pharmacies.

The proportion of meal sizes increased with 'supersizing'. With food cheaper to produce, manufacturers produced more food at a relative cost and remarked their meals as 'value meals'. This increased food and calorie intake significantly. By 1996, 25 per cent of the money customers spend on fast food was in supersize proportions.

In the late 1970s, advertisers started to target children. Again McDonald's was at the forefront in 1979 with the introduction of Ronald McDonald and their first 'Happy Meal which included a toy. The meal was specifically for children with a burger or nuggets, chips and a soft drink and contained more than 500 calories.

4. Socio-economic factors. There is a direct correlation between childhood obesity and parental education. Material education determines the choice of infant feeding methods with those more educated most likely to breastfeed and introduce solids from 6 months on which has a positive effect on Body Mass Index. Educated mothers are also more likely to access proper health care throughout their pregnancy and when children are young to provide healthier choices of food around this time. Mothers with higher education are also more likely to buy fresh produce including fruit and vegetables.

Poverty is also contributing to childhood obesity. Low-income families are more likely to live in areas with less access to parks and recreational areas and where there are less healthy eating options when eating out. Value for money is the rationale when eating out and fast food chains are the best option.

With such major changes in such a short time, it is no wonder childhood obesity is such an epidemic. It is our job as parents to take the reins now and realign our choices for cooking fresh meals at home rather than eating out too often, providing healthy options for snacks, slowing down in our 'hurry up' culture we have created so we don't have to rush through McDonald's drive through to get dinner into our children after the third extra-curricular activity for that day, choosing active, outdoor activities, rather than passive, indoor family activities like going to the park and family bike rides.

Micronutrient deficiency

Another key concern is the lack of essential micronutrients we are feeding our children. With the change in food pattern more towards packaged foods and take-outs, there are less of the dense micronutrients going into our children. This is impacting on our children's brain development and physical growth.

Cognitive development. Studies have shown that the food our children eat is having a direct effect on our children's brain development, cognition and mood disorders. This in turn has an effect on a child's behaviour, focus, ability to learn and concentration.

Do you remember from the mental resilience section of this book that in the first 2 years of our child's life, kids manufacture 80 per cent of their brain cells? This forms the basis of their brain capacity for the rest of their lives. Studies show that nutrients from the right foods act as triggers for the brain development process and so this is the time to help our kids build the trillions of connection that are happening in their brain right now.

Along with the synaptic development, the brain is an active organ in the body, which demands a high level of the daily energy requirements from the food we eat. For infants, 87 per cent of their daily intake supplies the brain and between the ages of 6-12, 30-45 per cent of energy is utilized in the brain. If we are providing our children with the right foods to create the energy needed, the brain will effectively be able to develop to its maximum capacity.

In a very simplified explanation, good nutrition (along with the right amount of sleep) facilitates the right chemical reactions in our child's brains necessary for cognitive development.

It is also thought that foods impact on our children's behaviour and there is current long-term studies looking at the effect of our change in diet on ADHD, behavioural issues and Autism. A poor diet could also contribute to mood disorders, anxiety and depression in children.

Physical growth. The height of our children is determined by genetics. However, for them to reach their maximum capacity we need to provide our children with the right nutrition to grow and develop.

These 5 main nutrients promote growth.

1. Calcium – maximizes bone growth and health keeping them strong into adulthood. This is especially essential in adolescents when the body forms half of its bone mass. Calcium is mostly found in dairy. Vitamin D is also important for the absorption of calcium.

2. Protein – being part of every single body tissue, protein helps build new cells and tissues and compounds that direct bodily processes, including enzymes and hormones. Proteins are mainly found in meat and eggs.

3. Fibre – this complex carbohydrate aids digestion and controls diabetes and cholesterol levels. It is important for transporting the right nutrients for the growth process.

4. Antioxidants – these battle the effects of free radicals, which can damage DNA as well as other cell parts. These are found in blueberries, broccoli, spinach, sweet potatoes and carrots.

5. Iron – red blood cells need iron to ferry oxygen to every cell in the body and it also plays a role in brain development and functioning. Meat including red meat, poultry and seafood as well as plant foods including spinach has the most iron.

Drinking plenty of water is also important to facilitate our children's growth.

12 WAYS TO PROMOTE HEALTHY EATING HABITS WITH YOUR KIDS

1. SET UP GOOD FOOD HABITS.

What to eat – by modeling healthy eating and providing nutritious meals, we are teaching our kids what they need to be physically resilience and develop strong, healthy bodies. Whatever we repeatedly feed our kids becomes habit of taste and texture so provide lots of variety and fresh fruit and vegetables. Teach about healthy foods versus sometimes foods and encourage your child to try every sort of different foods to see what they like. Remember it can take up to 28 times of trying a new food for it to become a habit.

When to eat – our children will be hungry every three to four hours. Help them determine hunger cues. Feed them a nutritious meal when they are hungry and don't force them to eat when they are not. Being in tune with their body will help them regulate a natural, healthy body weight. There is obviously a problem here if your child is eating all the time when they are not hungry or not eating at all even when they are hungry. If you are concerned at this point, seek medical advice.

How to eat – setting up the good manners of eating with your mouth, using a knife and fork (or spoon when they are much younger), elbows off the table, don't slurp the milk and say please and thank you for what you receive are standard habits we were taught as children. I bet when you sit around a dinner table now; you use some of the same rules that were used when you were a kid because they are habit. Think about what manners are important to you around food and instill them early. The manners will become a habit if reminded often enough. Another great habit might be to eat as a family at the dinner table.

Create food rituals – every family has a ritual around food and in fact, every culture and religion and even country has some sort of food ritual. What is your family ritual? Celebrate the eating of food at your family ritual and give thanks for where it has come from to nourish you and your family. Other rituals around food might happen at Christmas, Thanksgiving or at birthdays.

2. Less control, more fun

To celebrate and make eating a time of fun, relax the control at the dinner table. This will help your child learn when they are hungry or not and also stop the power struggles over food. As mentioned, food is a basic source of survival and when it becomes a situation of power, it loses it enjoyment and the bigger reason why we need food. Make dinnertime about family connection. Go around the table and do 'Favourite part of the day' or 'Say one thing you are grateful for today' or make up another inclusive family game that gives everyone a chance to feel a sense of significance and belonging. Eating should be shared in a positive environment so make dinner times fun rather than a constant battle.

3. Involve kids in the process

Kids love to be involved with the process of food. Grow some vegetables or herbs in the garden to use in your cooking. Planting, watering and nurturing a plant does far more good than just the nutritional value – it encourages empathy, compassion and teaches a child what is involved with growing what we eat on our plates. It helps children understand where our food comes from and there is something mystical and lovely about the paddock to plate idea when you can be involved. Let your kids cook in the kitchen.

My kids love to make cakes, cut up salad and fruit, make simple pasta dishes and create a huge mess that can easily be cleaned up. My daughter tells me it tastes better when she makes it and if that means she will eat more fruit and vegetables, it is a win-win for all involved. Take the kids to the supermarket and let them be involved with the buying of the food. Let them wheel the trolley and pick the apples. They could even suggest a dinner and then find the ingredients. Admittedly, if they are not used to doing this it might take longer and be noisier with them chattering, but embrace it. The kids will love it and you might even enjoy having them along for the supermarket journey.

4. Turn technology off

Make dinnertime a time for family connection. When else do we get to sit down and face each other and actually talk as a family? Block out any other distractions and make this a sacred family time – turn off the television and radio, don't allow phones or any other devices at the table and don't even allow toys at the table. Make it a time to really connect and enjoy the food together as a family.

5. Don't use bribes or rewards

How many times have you said 'If you eat all your dinner, you can have ice-cream for dessert?' If you have said it over 20 times, does it still work? What about over 100 times? Probably not. Your kids have wised up that even if they don't eat all their dinner, but their siblings do, they will still get ice-cream and if they don't finish their dinner and don't get ice-cream, it will not be the end of the world after the 100th time of you saying it. Bribes and rewards wear thin very quickly with kids. In addition, we want them to eat because they are hungry and it is a yummy dinner. If we bribe or reward them with external factors, they have no way of developing this intrinsic value.

6. **Cook with balance**
When you prepare a meal or school lunches, use foods from the 5 food groups. If you are feeding your child a good balance, you are preparing their bodies to be physically resilient and encouraging healthy eating habits.

7. **Make food from scratch at home as often as possible**
Take out foods and foods made with prepackaged ingredients are higher in calorie intake as well as salt and sugars. They can also contain shelf life preservatives and other colour preservatives that are not in the foods we cook from scratch. When you prepare a homemade meal, you control what goes in and can limit the calories, salt, sugar and preservatives.

Take pancakes for example. If you make them yourself, a basic batter recipe could be 1 cup of milk, 1 cup of wholemeal flour, 1 egg and a pinch of cinnamon. If you buy the pancake mix in a bottle a typical pancake mix has rice flour, maize flour, cane sugar, fructose, raising agents (450,500), flavour, salt, anticaking agent and vegetable gum (guar). Which one sounds healthier? Clearly the ones you made from scratch.

8. **Pack good school lunches**
Children are a captive audience at school. They have so much distraction that they will eat most things in their lunchbox so pack it well. Give children a variety of foods and make sure there is something in there from each of the main food groups. It is easy to stack it with prepackaged, 'filler foods' like bought cakes, muffins or biscuits, however if you are a little more creative, you can put in food that is high in nutrition and low in preservatives, sugars and carbohydrates.

9. You control the shopping

It always astounds me when parents tell me that their kids will only eat chicken nugget at home. The parents bought them in the first place and probably cooked them. Don't buy them and don't cook them. You control the shop. Whatever you put in the shopping trolley and cook your kids, especially when they are young is what they eat. Buy fresh produce. Buy diary. Buy protein. Buy carbohydrates. And make dinners and lunches from what you buy. If you don't want your kids to eat foods high in nitrates – don't buy bacon and ham, buy a chicken and roast it or cook chicken breasts instead. If you don't want your kids to eat 2 minute noodles, don't' buy them or chips or lollies or soft drink. Be creative in what you buy to satisfy the 5 food groups and just don't buy the rest.

10. Start as you mean to go on

If your child is less than 1 year old, now is the time to really think about what you want to feed them and start now. It is much easier to start now than try to break habits later. However, whatever age you start to implement a healthy eating regime is better than not starting at all. There will be an adjustment period if your children are older, but you can still achieve better habits by buying the foods you want to eat during this week's supermarket shop, rather than the food you always buy. Kids will eat the food eventually. If you are starting and your kids are older, go through the cupboards, fridge and freezer and get rid of the food you don't want your kids to eat then start a fresh with the food from this week's grocery shop. It is that easy to change a habit and then give it at least 6 weeks to stick for you and the kids.

11. Cook just one meal for dinner

When you have little children and they eat earlier than you, it is easy to fall into the trap of cooking two meals – a kid's meal and an adult's meal. It is not necessary. When your kids are under 12 months, you might have to puree their vegetables however it can just be your vegetables from that night put into the blender or even your whole dinner blended and fed to your child. Certainly from 1 or 2 years of age onwards, cook one meal and give your kids what you eat. They don't need bland food and the sooner they get used to eating the healthy foods you eat, the better.

12. Make fruit and vegetables accessible as snacks – limit high carbohydrate, high calorie snacks

Where do your kids go for snacks? What do you have in the 'snack place'? Do they go to a cupboard full of high carbohydrate, high salt/sugar snacks with no fresh produce? If so, change it up. Make it so that they only go to the fridge to get a snack such as dairy, a carrot or to the fruit bowl that is easily accessible. Make the cupboard harder to get to or just don't stock it as much the next time you shop. Put the rules in place about where snacks come from. Watch how quickly they either stop snacking or change to the more healthy option.

Common food issues: My child won't eat fruit and vegetables

Many families I have worked with tell me their children won't eat fruit and vegetables.

Here are some of the first questions to ask yourself if your kids won't eat fruit or vegetables:

Is it the texture? Kids, especially little kids don't like the soft, swishy textures of some fruit and vegetables. For example, the feel of bananas can put children off eating them, as can the wet feel of a kiwi fruit or mango.

Solution: Find another way to serve it up. Make a mango into an ice block. Blend frozen bananas and call it 'banana ice-cream'.

Is it the taste? Kids need to taste a food 28 times before they are converted to liking it. Did your child taste broccoli for the first time and say 'yuk' or 'yum'? Some of the fruits and vegetables can taste bland compared to other food items on their plate or those they are used to eating.

Solution: mix it. Mash it, blend it, grate it and include it in every meal that allows you to disguise it with the other flavours so it doesn't taste so bland as it does on its own. Keep on serving it, even if it is hidden with other flavours.

Do YOU eat fruit and vegetables? I was working with a family who didn't know how to make a salad and the husband had not eaten vegetables with his meat for years. The mum was dishing the vegetables up with the meat on the kid's plates, but not the Dads plate. Surprise, surprise, the kids didn't want to eat their vegetables because Dad didn't have to. If it is a regular occurrence to have a full fruit bowl and kids see you eat an apple – they will want one too. If you cut up and eat mango, rest assured they would want the juiciest bits. If you are eating avocado, they will think it is just the norm to eat it.

Solution: role model eating fruit and vegetables.

Are fruit and vegetables easily accessible? Do you have a big fruit bowl for kids to reach? Do you have cut up fruit in the fridge or serve it on a platter after dinner? How easy is it to reach for a piece of celery as opposed to a packet of chips? Again if you are in the habit of including it in every meal, it becomes the norm to eat it.

Solution: make fresh fruit and vegetables the number one choice to eat for snacks and have fruit and vegetables easily accessible. A fruit bowl in the middle of the bench or table, cut up carrots, celery or cucumber in the fridge or cut up melon in containers ready to eat.

What are dinner times like? Do you sit together as a family at the table and talk happily about the day? Or are dinner times stressful and the kids are made to sit at the dinner table until they have eaten everything on their plate including the last mouthful of cold broccoli or zucchini? When eating becomes a constant power struggle between the parents and the kids at the table, the fun evaporates and kids associate eating with a negative situation. The more the parents control the situation with eating the vegetables, the worse the situation will become and the less the children will eat.

When my mum was growing up, she was made to chew her meat 44 times before she swallowed it, there was no talking aloud and they children had to eat everything on their plate. It didn't make for fun family dinners.

Solution: don't control the situation. Serve up a meal that children are going to eat 80 per cent of it at least and make it fun. Don't threaten or bribe with dessert if they eat all of their dinner (see rewards and bribes on page xx for the reasons why they don't work). Start a family ritual of 'favourite part of the day' or a game that is fun. With distraction and not a focus on what the children are eating, you will be surprised how much they eat.

Common food issue: My child will only eat chicken nuggets

A mother at preschool one day was telling me her daughter would only eat chicken nuggets for dinner and she was complaining she had no room left in her freezer because it was full of chicken nuggets.

Do you see the problem here? The child was only eating chicken nuggets because that is what the mum was feeding her.

This same mum told me that any time she gave her child a different meal her daughter would complain so much that her mum would have to cook chicken nuggets. See another problem here? The little girl knew if she complained enough, her mum would cook her chicken nuggets. It was a win-win for the little girl every night, but not for the long term.

Solution: Don't buy chicken nuggets. Give your children the food you are having each night and if they refuse to eat it, don't cook another meal. Try all the tactics already mentioned and they will eventually eat when they are hungry. If you are concerned about your child at any time, consult your family doctor to work out a long-term solution.

COMMON FOOD ISSUE: MY KIDS ARE HUNGRY AT THE 'WRONG TIME'

On average, children are hungry every three to four hours, less if they are very active or under the age of 4 and this will not necessarily fit nicely into our adult eating habits of breakfast, lunch and dinner. When your kids are hungry, feed them. It is our job to have the right foods ready and available when they need to eat. The healthy pattern we develop here is eating when they are hungry and stopping when they are full. It is also important to fuel their bodies when they need it – it is a great way for them to learn to listen to their bodies and be in tune with what they need to feel energized.

CASE STUDY: HARRY AND HIS FOOD HABITS

A friend of mine has three children aged 6, 3 and a newborn. Harry is 3 and everyday he is hungry between 3pm and 5pm, right in that tricky time before dinner.

When you think about it, for an active 3-year-old boy who has had lunch at 12pm, there is a long time between lunch and dinner at 6pm. He was getting into the cupboard and eating snacks while his mum was busy with her fussy newborn. He was mostly eating biscuits or other carbohydrate snacks that were high in sugar and preservatives.

By dinner time at 6pm, it was no surprise Harry wasn't hungry. Dinnertime became a battle. The dad would sit there with him until he had eaten everything on his plate, alternatively they would bribe him to eat his dinner to get dessert. He would end up in tears and tantrums and dinnertime was not fun or enjoyable for anyone. The parents were trying to control what he was eating and when.

When the dinnertime wasn't working, my friend banned Harry from eating after 3pm so he would eat his dinner. This still didn't work. He was hungry at 4pm and his behaviour and mood would deteriorate, so that by the time he got to the dinner table at 6pm, he was now so cranky he wouldn't eat his dinner again. His parents would make him sit there until he had eaten all his dinner, which he didn't and so the power struggles and tantrums would happen all over again.

Problem: The parents were controlling his food intake. He knew when he was hungry and needed to eat and so went to the cupboard for snacks. He was eating 'fillers' at 4pm, which meant he didn't have room for a more nutritious meal at 6pm.

Solution: Feed Harry dinner at 4pm. Have a nutritious meal ready to go at 4pm that he can eat. When my kids were 3, 2 and a newborn, they ate their meal at 4pm and then sat back up at the dinner table with the whole family at 6pm to eat something small again. They wouldn't eat as much at actual dinnertime, but I was happy in the knowledge they had their nutritious meal at 4pm and any extra at 6pm was a bonus.

If you can not prepare a full meal by 4pm, cut up a plate of fruits and vegetables for your kids to snack on at 4pm. Add some hummus or other dip and make that their afternoon snack, rather than starchy, filler food from the cupboard. This will also probably make dinnertime more relaxed because you know your child has eaten their fruit and vegetables before dinner.

Also remember that wanting to eat all the time is on average a two week growth stage our children go through as they grow and develop and maybe it is just while they are on a growth spurt that you will need to provide an early dinner. By the age of 6 or 7, children can more easily wait between meals or simply have a light snack such as fruit to tied them over for dinner.

Our job as parents is to create a healthy food relationship for our children. It is also to develop healthy eating habits and patterns to promote growth and development and healthy weight gain. The routines, habits and behaviours we create for our children now around food will have a long lasting effect on their ability to prevent and bounce back from illness and disease now and into the future.

CHAPTER 18

Children need plenty of exercise

It is a given that kids need to be active. In fact, their bodies are wired to run, jump, skip, throw balls, flip, turn, climb and move. The younger they are, the more active they are. It is our job as parents to nurture this movement to allow them to maintain a healthy body weight, bounce back from illness or disease more easily, build strong bones and muscles, support healthy development of balance, movement and coordination and support brain development.

I was marking the roll in a class of 9 year olds the other day and I made a game that when I called out their name, they had to tell their class what their favourite activity was to do on the weekend. Out of the 12 boys, 6 of them said it was playing computer games and three of the boys said they spent hours every day on the weekend watching YouTube videos and playing Mine Craft. I pressed a little further and these kids didn't play sport on the weekends. Their parents were busy and they didn't own or ride bikes, go on walks or play outside. Alarm bells rang.

The same week, I watched a documentary on Forest Kindergartens in Denmark. This is where 4 and 5-year-old kids go to Kindergarten outside in the forest (as the name suggests) and there are 500 of them in Denmark alone. No matter the weather, they spend the whole day outside climbing trees, splashing in puddles, throwing sticks into the fiords or making kites out of bags and flying them along the flats.

So it seems that pockets of the world are getting it right when it comes to kids and exercise and we are still allowing kids to run free and move. However, this is certainly not the case in every pocket?

WHY AREN'T KIDS GETTING ENOUGH EXERCISE?

The reasons are consistent with why our children are getting more and more obese and unhealthy.

The perceived or real risks of letting our kids out on their bikes on their own. The change in leisure time as families and the propensity to stay at home and watch television, play computer games or go to the mall, rather than go on a family bike ride or do a sport.

Perhaps because more families are staying at home and leading life as a smaller family unit, the amount of opportunities to connect in the community over sport or vigorous activity has decreased. The old days of square dancing in the local hall are long gone and the local tennis club that used to be the hub of the town or suburb is no longer there. However, if you seek out the clubs in your areas to join and be part of as a family, they are still there and active in their own right. The local sailing club, football club, netball club or swimming pools are still alive in most communities.

The built environments in cities are not necessarily conducive to an active lifestyle. Bike lanes, parks and playgrounds and open spaces for kicking the football are few and far between. The cities that do well (places like Washington DC) have an integral bike lane system that spreads for miles and miles in each direction of the town and every weekend there are hundreds of families together riding bikes. In Australia, Canberra has similar bike paths away from the roads to promote activity. In each of these cities, there is plenty of parkland to explore for hikes and family walks and picturesque lakes or rivers. In Sydney, the Bondi to Bronte walk and the extensive opportunity to use the beautiful beaches are also supportive of an active lifestyle.

The key to being an active family is to look in *your* area to find the kid friendly spaces, like bike paths, parks and sports ovals. If the spaces are not there, actively lobby to get a local playground or space for kids to run and play. A local mum, Claudia Bowman lobbied to get a playground built in a disused area of a park and after many road blocks it happened. The suburb of Sydney's Kings Cross has a history for being notorious for it's nightlife and illicit undertakings. However, in the past five years there has been a boom in the number of families living in the area because it is close to the city and good schools. With the changing face of the area, Claudia knew that it was the corner of the park where dealings took place and homeless people slept, however she saw potential to reuse the space to cater for the families that had moved in. After many hurdles with the local council, they finally agreed to build the playground. Now, every weekend hundreds of families use the space. An instant community has formed for families and it has created the opportunity for kids to play safely together in the outdoors with climbing frames, swings and slippery dips.

Another major and disturbing factor limiting exercise in our kids is that physical education (PE) is not mandated in every school in many countries. In the US, only 6 states mandate 60 minutes of physical activity at school for their kids each day.

When we lived in the US, the school my children attended did not incorporate physical education (PE) into the curriculum. It was at the discretion of the teacher and so when it was -8 C degrees outside for 4 months and then 40 C degrees + in summer and 90 % humidity, the teacher did not actively choose to take the kids out to sport. Added to this was that they ate in the cafeteria for lunch and in the classroom for recess because it was too cold or too hot which meant they hadn't been outside all day. So by the time my children got home, they were like caged lions. They had been inside all day and needed to run and move.

In Australia under the new National Curriculum, it does mandate for 60 minutes of physical activity per week but again, this is mostly up to the teachers. The school my children go to now values sport and exercise and incorporates it in everything they do. There are two dedicated sport days where they do sport for at least 60 minutes across the two days. They also run lunch clubs for all of the major sports and often have two games of football or soccer playing on the ovals at lunchtime refereed by the teachers. They often do a 2 km run at the beginning of the day before they start their lessons and have at least two sport days each term dedicated to swimming, running, athletics, football or netball. While they are mostly exhausted by the end of the week, they are learning well, settled in their class and loving the opportunity to be outdoors, playing sport.

How much exercise do children need?

The guidelines are very similar across USA, UK and Australia with the recommendation that children aged 0 to 5 years should be active for at least three hours every day spread throughout the day. For children aged 5 to 12 years, 60 minutes or more of physical activity is recommended EACH DAY.

Children aged 5 to 12 years need to do exercise that muscles and bones as well as maintaining and increasing fitness levels.

This is broken up into the following categories:

AEROBIC ACTIVITY – it should make up the majority of the 60 minutes and includes moderate intensity activity like walking to school, bike riding or playing at the park, or vigorous-intensity activity such a running, swimming, dancing or most team sports. The other recommendation is the vigorous-intensity aerobic activity is required on at least 3 days per week

MUSCLE STRENGTHENING – this helps the muscles to grow and develop and includes such things as climbing trees, doing the monkey bars at the playground or gymnastics. It might also be games of tug of war and for older kids push-ups, sit-ups or weights.

BONE STRENGTHENING – this keeps the bones active and makes them stronger to avoid breaks and fractures. This might be skipping, running, playing hopscotch, gymnastics or bouncing on the trampoline.

PRACTICAL WAYS TO GET YOUR KIDS MOVING

From toddlers to teens, it is really our job as parents to help kids form a healthy relationship around exercising. We want to instill good habits and routines for them to maintain a healthy body weight and to be active when they are older.

Exercise with a 2 year old does not mean making them jog around the block, nor does it mean getting a 9 year old on a treadmill – it means making them move.

Here are some practical ways to get kids moving.

1-3 YEARS. At this age, children need 3 hours of activity across the day. If you have sat and watched a 1 to 3 year old child, it can seem is as though they never stop moving. I was at the sports carnival looking after one of my friends two year old for about 45 minutes. He got up and down in my arms maybe 30 times, chased a dog a few times, ran after a couple of little friends, ran 50-metres in the toddlers race, followed his brother up and down the track; he did not stop moving for the whole 45 minutes.

Here are some suggestions to reach the three hours:

- Walk around the block (30 minutes)
- Chase bubbles around the backyard (30 minutes)
- Walk up the front stairs three times (30 minutes)
- Free play/crawling time around (30 minutes)
- Play chasings around the yard (20 minutes)

- Walk up the hall to the bath (10 minutes)
- Bounce on the trampoline (30 minutes)

It is pretty simple and easy to get a 1 to 3 year old moving. The key is to not keep them in the stroller (pram) when you go somewhere but to get them out of the stroller and spend 20 minutes holding their hand to walk along or letting them crawl or walk on the grass outside or even around the house. The concern at this age can be that they will fall over and hurt themselves. While it is important to be vigilant with supervision, know that they will fall but they will get back up again. Kids at this age are resilient and bounce back quickly after falling down.

Other ideas might be to chase a ball or balloon around the house or yard, crawl on the beach, have a play date with another toddler, go for a swim together or go to an age-appropriate park. You are building the foundation around a healthy, active lifestyle and role modeling that play and exercise is an important part of your child's day.

3-5 YEARS. By the time children are 3-5 years of age, they are often in organized care or at least preschool a couple of days a week. There should be ample opportunity for kids to play with their friends at the centre and preferably OUTDOOR play.

The days when they are home with you, here are some ideas to reach 3 hours of physical activity:

- Go to the park and actively engage with your child 1 hour
- Walk to and from the park 30 minutes
- Have a running race in the backyard or hallway 30 minutes
- Play kick and chase with a ball 30 minutes
- Bounce on the trampoline 30 minutes

Kids at this age have a lot of energy and will need to run, jump, hop, skip and just move generally to tire themselves out for their afternoon or nighttime sleep. Any outdoor activity is great and if you are inside for the day, run up the hall, walk up steps or play active games like 'ring a ring a rosy'. This is also an age where extra curricular activities start in many places and you could incorporate a ballet class or soccer into the week. Swimming lessons are also important at this age to instill water confidence. However, there is no need to go overboard as they are still forming their habits and relationship with being active. Again at this age, we are building the habit of scheduling exercise into our kid's days and allowing them to build a fun, loving relationship with being active.

5-12 YEARS. There are so many opportunities to get kids to be active and it is important to incorporate scheduled activities along with time for non-scheduled activities (For example, just playing). There is nothing more fun than seeing kids play and enjoy being active at this age.

Depending on your child's strengths and skills, there are plenty of organized extra-curricular activities such as dance, soccer, netball, tennis, gymnastics, futsal, football, karate and swimming that each last for an hour or so. While these are important and good fun, don't rely on just these activities for exercise.

The main aim is that kids enjoy their sport. Too many times sport becomes a competitive pastime for parents, more so than for the kids at this age and they feel the pressure to perform and compete. Mostly, kids just want to have fun and enjoy being with their friends at their soccer or netball game. While it is important to develop skills, it is not necessarily the kid's objective.

Recently at school, the Kindergarteners had their first-ever running carnival. The kids were excited and a little nervous with anticipation about what happens at a running carnival. Most of the kids were oblivious to the winning and losing aspect and just wanted to get out there and run. However, a lot of the parents I spoke to were already feeling and anticipating the disappointment for the kids if they came last and how they might cope with it. The thing to remember here is that kids live very much in the moment and it isn't their worry, it is the parents putting their own schema of losing in races or being embarrassed for their child if they come last in front of everyone who is watching.

This is also evident on the side of the netball courts when mums and dads yell at their kids to try harder or do better or catch better or shoot better. The kids just want to play their game and have fun at this age and not necessarily care about being the best or winning the game. It is about participating and setting up a healthy relationship with sport – rather than forcing our children to win.

Non-scheduled activities are important here too. It's a time when children get to use their imagination and generate their own fun. This might include riding bikes, scooters or skateboards, bouncing on a trampoline, going to the park, walking the dog, running races with friends, kicking the football, climbing trees, having a swim at the beach, lake or river, backyard cricket or at the local nets, any free play time or meeting friends for an active, outdoor play date. This is where children learn intrinsically that exercise is important and how you can set them up to be active. The best activities are child-led, not parent-directed where children set up the rules and the game. They are not only being active, they are learning independence, how to deal with conflict, negotiation skills and having their own fun.

More and more families are choosing to live in apartments or houses with no backyards for convenient proximity to schools and shops. If this is your family, it takes a more concerted effort to get out and move. Make time to the kids to the park or out of the house and let them run around to get their 60 minutes. The walk to the park might be 15-20 minutes of the 60 minutes. It is essential to get out and be active every day to be fit and healthy.

Kids who are active benefit in so many ways including developmentally, socially, mentally and physically. Not only are they getting the necessary fitness and healthy body weight but it also helps children get outdoors to appreciate their natural surrounds and soak up the beauty. While they are outside, they are getting vitamin D from the sun and breathing in fresh, healthy air that is good for mental development and wellbeing, as well as for physical health too.

CHAPTER 19

Make good hygiene a habit

The last building block of physical resilience is teaching our children good hygiene. Good hygiene is important for maintaining health, cleanliness and preventing illness and disease.

Here are some personal hygiene habits and ways to remind our children to practice them regularly:

1. WASHING HANDS – Teaching kids how to wash their hands and when to wash them is important to ward off spreading infection. Kids should wash their hands before food, when preparing food, after they have been to the toilet or blown their nose and when they have come in from outside, especially if they have been touching animals. Have a reminder on the door of the bathroom, remind them before they eat and send them to the bathroom regularly to wash their hands when necessary, so it becomes a habit. Make sure the soap is accessible and that your children can reach the taps.

2. BRUSHING TEETH – Kids should brush their teeth twice a day, once in the morning before they leave the house and once at night before bed. This helps with teeth hygiene as well as bad breath. Make it fun – get electric toothbrushes, fun toothpaste that tastes good, set a timer and make sure they are doing it properly. Have mouthwash and floss available should the kids need it for that day.

3. BODY WASHING – This varies between cultures and beliefs. However, for your kids to get into a habit of staying clean, you need to set up a regular schedule for baths/showers. If it is every day, be consistent and make sure it happens every day. Provide the soap and washers (if you use them) and teach children early about the parts that need washing the most. Remind children who are 8 years and older to wash under their arm pits as from this age, they start producing the chemicals in sweat that produce body odour. Encourage the use of deodorant when it is required.

4. WEARING CLEAN CLOTHES – Wash and insist on clean clothes. Unwashed clothes, especially underwear and socks carry bacteria. Establish with your children what gets washed every time they wear it (for example, socks, undies and t-shirts.) Pajamas might be OK for two nights depending on your own beliefs around cleanliness and how much your children sweat at night. Get your children involved with folding and hanging out the laundry or putting it in the dryer from an early age.

5. GOING TO THE TOILET – Wiping and hygiene around using the toilet is important to prevent spread of infection. For girls, it is important to wipe from front to back to reduce bacteria causing bladder infections. For boys, do they wipe after urinating or drip dry? How much toilet paper do they use? You establish the hygiene around the toilet. Reiterate strongly to wash their hands after going to the toilet and to flush. If you insist on the lid down, teach them that, too.

6. CLEAN LINEN – Regularly wash sheets and towels. They also carry bacteria and can harbour other parasites like worms and even nits can stay alive for a while in sheets. Have a regular schedule and let your children know what it is so they can help with the process. If it is every two weeks for sheets, get them to take the sheets off. It might be every week for towels so on Friday night (or more regularly), they put their towels in the wash.

7. **BLOWING NOSES AND COUGHING** – Teach your kids how to blow their nose from the age of about 3 or 4 and put their tissues in the bin. This stops infection spreading from tissues or snot. Picking your nose is also not on for the risk of infecting others with illness and because well, snot is just disgusting. Children can learn to cough into their arm or elbow to avoid spreading germs.

8. **CLEANLINESS AROUND FOOD** – Explain the direct route of germs and bacteria being carried from food into the mouth and then into the body to your children. I was teaching a lesson on diseases at school and how to avoid them to a group of 8 year olds. When the topic came up on how easy it is to eat a germ that's transferred from hands to the food, the kids were horrified and lots of noises of disgust ensued. These kids will be washing their hands from now on. Hand washing before touching food is important. It is also good for kids to know about safe handling of food – cold foods need to be stored in the fridge so don't leave the milk on the counter; chicken and other meats need to be cooked through before being eaten, fruit and vegetables should be washed before being consumed, meat should be cut on a separate board to vegetable and fruit and whatever other rule you have in your house around food and hygiene.

Instilling good hygiene habits will prevent diseases and illnesses and also help children know what to focus on for cleanliness and hygiene when illness *does* strike so it is not spread to others.

CHAPTER 20

A typical day in the life of a healthy child

A child that is healthy is getting enough sleep, enough good nutrition, enough exercise and has learnt good hygiene habits. They also know the habits, expectations and routine in the household to help them with their sleeping, eating, exercising and hygiene. Here is what I have seen works with children to maintain a healthy, active lifestyle.

TODDLER 1-3 YEARS

Case study: 2 years old Sophie

Sophie is 2 years old. She has two siblings aged 6 months and 5 years and this is how she leads an active lifestyle.

Sophie wakes at about 6.30am. She has Weetbix with strawberries for breakfast and watches a little bit of Dora while her mum gets her big brother ready for school. Sophie knows she is only allowed to watch two Dora shows before the iPad goes off and there is no television in the mornings. She then goes into the yard with her big brother and they blow bubbles and chase them while her mum is feeding her 6-month-old sister.

When they are ready (hair brushed, clothes on, teeth brushed, shoes on) they walk to school.

There is a double pram, room enough for Sophie and her baby sister. At school, Sophie gets out of the pram and follows her big brother around the playground. She chases a ball that has escaped from a game. When the bell rings, she says goodbye and Sophie and her mum and sister go across the road to the playground to meet one of the other mums and Sophie's friend.

Sophie and her friend go up and down the slide, swing on the swing with their mums pushing, play running around the playground and have another go on the slide. At 10am, it is time to walk home again. Sophie doesn't want to sit in her pram so her mum holds her hand and walks her home.

At home again Sophie has a snack of biscuits with cheese and some cut up apple with a sippy cup of water. She then has free playtime in her playroom and builds block towers. She goes outside again and plays with the dog and then comes in and it is almost time for lunch. While her baby sister is having another feed, Sophie plays with her toys.

At 12pm, Sophie has lunch. Sometimes she will have a sandwich with chicken, cheese, grated carrot and lettuce along with cut up fruit, but today she is having spaghetti bolognese from last night. She has another drink of her water and eats her lunch with her mum.

At 1pm, Sophie is so tired from her morning she has her afternoon sleep until 2.30pm.

When she wakes, Sophie has a homemade choc chip and banana muffin to take in the pram with her while they walk down to pick up her big brother from school. She gets out of the pram at school and has a play with the big kids on the equipment.

They get home at 4pm: Sophie and her brother play for an hour. At 5pm, they have a bath. At 6pm they have dinner. Tonight they are having a chicken stir-fry with rice. At 7pm, Sophie reads a story with her dad, brushes her teeth and is in bed with the lights out by 7.30pm.

During this day, Sophie might have had a couple of tantrums about getting in the pram or going to bed in the day time, cried a few times and talked to her baby sister. She had lots of cuddles with her mum and they sang songs together throughout the day. She might have also watched an episode of the Wiggles or played a game on the iPad for 20 minutes.

There has been a balance of good nutrition, exercise, sleep and good hygiene throughout her day. There has also been a good balance of habits, routines and expectations around technology and positive discipline. Sophie has also had varied experiences playing outdoors and indoors, interacting with friends and bonding with her siblings.

Preschooler 3-5 years

Case study: 4 years old Jack

Jack is 4 years old and is at his last year of preschool. He has been going 2 days a week for the past two years and loves his days at preschool to see his friends and play in the sandpit.

Today, Jack is at home with his mum. He is an only child. This is what a typical day at home for Jack looks like.

Jack gets up at about 6.30am and the first thing he does is go to the toilet and then goes back to his room to get dressed before he heads to the kitchen. He is old enough to choose his own clothes and loves his new t-shirt with a pair of blue shorts. He can dress himself, although he needs mum to do the button up on his t-shirt.

Jack is hungry when he wakes up, so his Dad is cooking him bacon and eggs this morning with two pieces of wholemeal toast. He eats with his Dad while his mum is getting ready.

When Jack finishes breakfast, he gets his cars out and makes a full racetrack with them. By now it is 8am and he is getting excited about meeting his buddy at the park at 9am. Jack brushes his teeth, goes to the toilet and makes his bed.

Jack's mum has packed him a lunch box with a mandarin, cut up celery and carrot sticks, an apricot muesli bar and a piece of home-made chocolate cake. It also has his water in it. Jack knows he can snack on this until they get home.

Jack has bought his soccer ball to the park and when he meets his friend they take the ball and kick is around for about 20 minutes. Then they come into the playground and play on the swings, the slide and monkey bars; he loves this park because there is a really tall octopus climbing frame. Jack and his friend climb to the top. When they climb down, they play a game of tip with some new friends they have made at the park that day and they all run through the playground having fun.

By 11am, it is time to finish at the park and go home. Jack doesn't want to say goodbye to his friend so he cries leaving the park. His mum cuddles him and reassures him they will see each other again.

When they get home, Jack washes his hands and then has some lunch. While mum is preparing lunch, Jack is allowed to go on his iPad for 20 minutes to play his favourite game. When his lunch is ready, Jack sits up with his mum and eats his lunch. Today he has a wrap with cream cheese, ham off the bone, lettuce and tomato. His mum knows he likes cucumber and celery so she cuts some up for the side of his plate. He has his water to drink as well.

It is now 1pm and Jack decides it is time to play Lego. He builds a tall tower and puts it next to the racetrack he was playing with this morning. It is fun building Lego towers. He then reads a story with his mum and helps her fold the washing.

At 2.30pm, Jack's mum needs to go the supermarket to do the grocery shopping and Jack's job is to push the trolley. He loves this job and is getting better and better at it. He doesn't like when mum touches it, but sometimes she needs to so he doesn't hit into anyone. Jack also helps mum put the groceries in.

By 4pm, Jack and his mum are home again. Jack goes outside

with his mum and kicks the ball around. He sees one of the neighbours out there and his little friend comes over for them to kick the ball together.

At 5pm, Jack has a bath. At 6pm, Jack has his dinner. Tonight he is having a piece of salmon with cous cous and stir fried vegetables – his favourite. He loves talking to Dad and Mum at the dinner table. He will also have a glass of milk.

At 7pm, Jack starts his bedtime routine. He reads a story with Dad or Mum, packs away his cars and Lego, brushes his teeth, goes to the toilet and then the lights go out between 7.30pm and 7.45pm.

As an only child, Jack is getting a good balance between playing on his own and playing with others. He is getting outdoor play as well as indoor, imaginative play with his cars and his Legos. He knows the rules and habits in the house and abides by them around technology, snacks and good hygiene.

School aged 5-12 years

Case study: Hudson family
(Jeremy 11 years, Sarah 9 years, Ben 7 years)
The Hudson family live near the beach and their life is focused around it. The kids all wake up between 6.30am and 7am and go down to the beach with their Dad. They go for a swim, Jeremy sometimes goes for a surf and they play in the sand. Their dog also likes going down to the beach and one of them have to take it for a walk along the beach each morning.

When they get home, each have a bowl of cereal (generally Weetbix or porridge) and a piece of wholemeal toast with cheese. Sometimes they have a glass of juice but generally they have water with their breakfast.

They then get dressed for school in their bedrooms. Even Ben knows where his school clothes are and puts them on for the day.

Once the kids have brushed their teeth and hair, they make their beds and put their shoes on.

At 8am, the Hudson family leaves the house to go to school. While they are at school, Ben and Jeremy love playing football at lunch time with their friends on the oval and Sarah usually plays handball at lunch. Two days a week, they have PE during class time and, today, Jeremy has football for an hour and half after school. Mum picks Ben and Sarah up and they sometimes go out for afternoon tea to the local bakery for a treat and then go to the park next door to Jeremy's oval. They get something for Jeremy too because he is always hungry after football.

Mum packed this lunch this morning and put in a chicken and salad sandwich, cut up carrot, celery and cucumber, a yoghurt, a homemade ham, cheese and zucchini muffin and a Cruskit with peanut butter on it. Sometimes Mum also packed them pasta with bolognese sauce or sushi every Tuesday.

Every Wednesday, all three kids do swimming in the afternoon, on Tuesday Sarah does dance and Ben does surfing. When mum works, the kids go to after school care.

As soon as the kids get home, they do their homework. On days when they have things on after school, they don't get as much done.

At 6pm, the kids have their showers and baths so they are washed and clean and ready for dinner.

Dinner is served between 6.30pm and 7pm, depending on what time Dad gets home. Dinner tonight is a BBQ with steak, sausages and chicken kebabs with a green salad.

After dinner, the kids play outside for a while or play a game together inside.

The kids know they need to get their bags ready for the next day at school, brush their teeth and go to the toilet before they go to bed. They like to go to bed and read before the lights go out and sometimes their parents read to them. Lights are out by 8.30pm.

During the week, there is no time for technology other than when it is used for homework so they know that on Fridays, they can spend time on technology if they want to after school because they have nothing else on those days.

The Hudson's know the boundaries, expectations and habits in their house. They are incorporating the beach into their active lifestyles and are eating and sleeping well. They also have time to enjoy a good balance of scheduled and unscheduled time. This allows the Hudson's time to play together and bond as a family.

CONCLUSION

Call to Action

Children are born with an ability to become resilient. Humans are wired to bounce back from adversity and difficulty.

However, the real ability and skill to bounce back lies in how we are raised as children and the way our resilience is nurtured and shaped by the experiences, memories and relationships we form with parents, siblings, teachers, carers and other influencers.

When I was growing up, we were given the opportunities to fail and make mistakes on our own. We were given the opportunity to develop our own coping mechanisms and skills to overcome challenges and adversities.

Parenting styles were different and raising children was largely done as a community or a village. Kids were allowed to explore the world on their own in their safe village while developing independence and courage.

The time we live in now and the way we raise our children has changed.

As a parent collective, we are somewhat better now at understanding and teaching emotions to our kids and we know that having skills and tools to deal with these emotions are a big part of bouncing back from adversity.

However, many other elements of parenting have slipped and as a result, we are raising our kids to be less resilient.

With helicopter parenting in full force and our lack of ability to let our kids go, to be the independent beings they were meant to be, we are stifling their coping mechanisms. Law mowing parenting is now all the rage where which parents clear the path of problems for their children and they no longer experience the ups and downs of life. This means children can not develop the skills to deal with disappointment, relationships or struggles in the classroom which is not setting them up for a successful life that is full of ups and downs.

This is not necessarily the fault of our own parenting skills. In Carl Honore's words, it is society's pressure to 'push, polish, protect and project' our children so they are 'ready for the world' that is causing an unbalanced relationship in raising a resilient child.

While we think we are raising strong children by pandering to their every need and being there 24/7, we are actually stifling, smothering and wrapping our children in cotton wool. It is counterproductive and actually negatively affective their ability to thrive and flourish in a challenging world.

Think about this:

- Of the children in front of us right now, 1 in 4 will suffer from anxiety and depression in their life. Maybe higher by the time they become adults. And, right now, 1 in 5 of these children are already experiencing a mental illness. I have seen first hand the effects of anxiety and depression in kids. It is hard enough for adults to find the coping skills and mechanisms; it is almost impossible for children.
- Of these same children, 30 per cent will be obese with obesity being the number one childhood epidemic sweeping the Western world.
- Sadly, researchers have called it that our children will be the first generation to have a shorter lifespan than their parents and grandparents.

- Children's persistence and problem solving skills are at an all time low – I see this all too often when I am teaching. Children give up when they can't tie their shoelaces or when they can't do a mathematical problem.
- Emotional intelligence is also low and desperately needed in our children right now as a tool to help them navigate the school playground or social media scene with courage and bravery.

The exciting thing is, as parents to these children now, we have the power to change these facts and statistics. We have the resources and skills to build strong, resilient kids who will maintain a healthy weight, be mentally well, fight back from illness and disease to live as long as us and learn invaluable persistence and problem solving skills as well as emotional intelligence. We have the resources to help our kids thrive and flourish.

Along with the propensity to molly coddle our kids, we are also living in a 'hurry up' culture where we are running from one activity to the next to give our child the opportunity to be next Olympian or Wallaby, without nurturing their down time.

We are shuffling kids out the door to get to school, work, extra-curricular activities and life is moving at an ever-increasing pace. 'Hurry up' has become our new word. 'Hurry up' and get your shoes on. 'Hurry up' and eat your breakfast. 'Hurry up' and go to bed.

Kids need to slow down to develop and grow.

They need time to play, imagine and create.

They need time to eat well, sleep well and kick the ball around the back yard.

They need time to live in the moment – because this is where they are at naturally.

Raising children today is about getting the tricky balance right of parenting for the future, while meeting children in the now.

Our children are not thinking about tomorrow's meeting or yesterday's disaster. They are not thinking about how hard it is to get out the door by 7am so we can be in the boardroom for our first meeting or work commitment. They are not even thinking about putting their shoes on or brushing their teeth at 6.30am. They are captured in the moment by the shiny thing that is in front of them. They are most probably wondering how that shiny thing got there and if it had wings, could it fly or, if it had feet, could it walk across the playroom floor. Their minds are figuring out how to live in the world and they are about to ask one of the 397 questions that they ask everyday to make sense of this shiny thing and the world around them.

We are doing our children a disservice by allowing them to be caught up in the treadmill of life, the constant pace and movement that society has deemed is necessary to 'keep up with the Jones'.

Our children live in the moment and we must meet them there. This is the place we can really connect with our children and build the strong, solid relationship with us that our children need to be resilient.

The best news is that we can stop the tide.

As parents, we have the power to slow down.

We have the power to feed our children the nutritious food they need to grow and develop into strong adults.

We have the power to provide them with the best education to build strong minds.

We have the power to let our kids experience freedom and independence to learn how to fail.

We have the power to create the memories our children will have and build a positive, fun schema around life's events and activities.

We are also the adults who build the strong, solid relationships with our children to help them feel a sense of connection, belonging and significance.

If we really meet the child we have in front of us, rather than the child we want or expect, we can pour our love, energy and emotion into that child so they are loved, supported and nurtured to grow and develop into the best versions of themselves.

Our children are little for such a short time. Between the ages of zero and two years, our children embed 80 per cent of their brain development that will carry them for the rest of their lives. We have the power to influence how they develop their brain and body and, for that, we need to take charge and make a change.

We need to ensure our children are physically, emotionally and mentally resilient to fight the battles life throws at them and succeed. We want them to be active citizens and strong adults who are able to bounce back after stress and adversity and we want them to be brave, independent and curious to interact with their world.

We need to find the balance in raising our children to be strong, resilient and confident adults so they can weather the ups and downs of life and thrive, not just survive… let's get started!

ACKNOWLEDGMENTS

Without the extraordinary connections I have made with parents and children, this book would have been impossible to write. I have been fortunate to have a front row seat to the hearts and minds of humanity in all its forms. Thank you for sharing your journey with me; it has been the greatest pleasure and privilege.

My family, Tony, Zoe, Lachie and Maddie, inspire me everyday to be a better person and have taught me everything I know about being a parent. They know how to journey the ups and downs of life, create everlasting memories and share in the joy of life. As a military family, resilience has always been at the forefront of every move or change and has held us together when times were tough.

My book editor, Anjanette Fennell inspired and coached me to write this book and I am forever grateful for her guidance and belief in me, often when I didn't have it in myself. When I told her I had this idea to write a book about resilience in children, but no time, her support was unwavering. I was teaching full time with three little kids and my husband was away for six months. Her premise was just write for one hour a day. Set a timer whenever you have a spare hour and just write – before the kids woke up, after they went to bed, before dinner when they were happy – one hour a day is all it took to write a book!

I wrote 10,000 words a week and wrote my book in seven weeks. Thank you for being there right when you were, Anj. You are truly inspirational.

There were many, many influencers along the way and I would like to thank people who I interviewed, turned to for advice on resilience and book writing or talked to through the process; Graham Long, Maggie Dent, Dannielle Miller, Emma Grey, Dr Lea Waters, Carl Honore, Dr Arne Rubinstein, Dr Kristy Goodwin, Hilary Shelton, Cathie & Rob Harris, David Scott and Dr Jane Nelsen. I would like to make special mention of my Number 1 loyal supporter, Andrew Mierisch who was the best man at my wedding and is my husband's best friend. His constant words of encouragement and ongoing conversations even before the book was written, right down to choosing my book cover has been unwavering – thank you. I also want to make special mention of his wife Karen Eck and daughter Jazz for their wise counsel and great ideas. Thank you also to my book publisher, Maureen Cutajar who made this book a reality.

And to you, who has just read this book. Thank you for raising resilient, confident, emotionally intelligent children who can face the world and all it throws at them. Thank you for raising active citizens who contribute to the world when we are long gone and the cycle of raising children in a positive way continues.

www.annapartridge.com

www.ingramcontent.com/pod-product-compliance
Lightning Source LLC
Chambersburg PA
CBHW030252010526
44107CB00053B/1679